Praise for the Work of B. H. Fairchild

"Lush with cottonwoods, Kansas autumns, Ford tractors, dust devils, oil rigs, family and the pull of history, B. H. Fairchild's poems resonate with loneliness, like the wide-open plains and small towns where he sets so many of them. . . . Fairchild speaks for anyone who has yearned to escape over the horizon [capturing] the unnamable longing that creeps into ordinary lives and slowly snuffs out youthful dreams. It is history, writ large and small, that beats strong through *Early Occult Memory Systems of the Lower Midwest*. . . . This is the American voice at its best: confident and conflicted, celebratory and melancholic."
　　　　　　　　　　　　　—Michael Hainey, *New York Times*

"B. H. Fairchild is one of those poets prose readers love: Meaty, maximalist, driven by narrative, he stakes out an American mythos in which the personal and the collective blur. . . . [A] lack of sentimentality infuses *Usher*, an insistence on seeing things as they really are. That's a vivid and compelling strategy, for at the heart of these poems is the issue of longing, of what we want and yet can never have."
　　　　　　　　　　　　　—David Ulin, *Los Angeles Times*

"[The poems in *Early Occult Memory Systems of the Lower Midwest*] are an ecstatic celebration of language—long, lavish lines sprawling across the page as the speaker's consciousness roams the Kansas countryside. Fairchild is a spinner of tales who writes unforgettably of loneliness and the tenderness of the Midwest."
　　　　　　　　　　　　　—Elise Paschen, *Chicago Tribune*

"I daresay [Fairchild] has arrived with some of the future of American poetry in his hands. It satisfies this reader to know that someone so steady is running the machine."

—Christopher Bakken, *Contemporary Poetry Review*

"Fairchild's ability not only to choose a story but to pace it and to reveal its meaning through the unfolding of the narrative is probably unmatched in contemporary American poetry. The incisive psychology, the vividly descriptive diction, the large repertoire of vocabulary, the weightiness of his settings and plots: all these contribute to the delightful sensation that one is reading, simultaneously, the best poetry and best prose. I cannot think of another living poet capable of delivering such pleasure. . . . Not since James Wright has there been a poet so skilled at representing the minds and imaginations of ordinary American working people."

—Kate Daniels, *Southern Review*

"The energetic and vivid poems of *Usher* are a delight . . . even those who approach poetry with trepidation will be mesmerized."

—Deb *Jurmu, Sacramento Book Review*

"*Usher* should solidify B. H. Fairchild's reputation as an essential force in contemporary letters. The praise he receives typically includes 'American,' suggesting a smaller audience than he deserves. He merits acclaim beyond the academy, beyond our shores."

—Barbara Berman, *The Rumpus*

"The more one studies Fairchild's poems, the more his intelligence surfaces along with his more obvious compassion. I have no trouble ranking him with the best poets of his generation."

—David Mason, *Hudson Review*

"Fairchild's singular distinction is his ability to make people and incidents in his work more actual than any, it seems, in any other kind of writing."   —*Booklist*

"With elegance and restrained subtlety, Mr. Fairchild interweaves topics that become something like musical themes, including the central theme of machine work. . . . Anyone who can lay claim to the authorship of this much excellent poetry wins my unqualified and grateful admiration."   —Anthony Hecht

" 'The ache of thwarted desire' and its mysterious and uncanny attachment to the people and landscape of southwest Kansas has been one of the abiding preoccupations of B. H. Fairchild's poetry, and the trajectory it has traced over the past thirty years has inscribed one of the most colorful, exact, and memorable idioms into American poetry. What Sherwood Anderson, E. A. Robinson, and James Wright mined from their locales, Fairchild has perfected from his Oklahoma Panhandle, and that is to show that no matter how isolated in time and space, no matter how cut off from its dreams, the human spirit persists in believing that it is 'on the edge of something, something rare.' *The Blue Buick* is a magnificent and important addition to the grain of American poetry."
—Michael Collier, author of *An Individual History*

"This book gathers essential poems from B. H. Fairchild's epic exploration of contemporary American masculinity. He depicts the vexations of class and labor with the 'tonnage of a full body / slam' and 'a kind of wonder / bodied forth.' Virtuosic narratives, portraits and quiet lyrics offer 'the heart's dream / of art's divinity,' as they illuminate myths and heroes, gritty realities and triumphal moments of insight. I cherish these poems for their supple elegance and felt wisdom."   —Robin Becker, author of *Tiger Heron*

"In the middle of the twentieth century, the poet James Wright asked, 'Where is the sea, that once solved the whole loneliness / Of the Midwest?' Throughout his career, the indispensable poet B. H. Fairchild has answered, with that other great Midwesterner T. S. Eliot, 'The sea is all about us.' That is the sea of estrangement—from roots, from class, from childhood and family. Fairchild's is an old story, but one that Americans have often had trouble telling, unlike their European counterparts. He tells it realistically, musically, and occasionally with that nostalgia which marks him as American. His unique power is in leading his dead from the field of personal memory and into the living history of the poem. We have had poets like this—Randall Jarrell, James Wright, Richard Hugo—inheritors of the legacy of Robert Frost. At this time, B. H. Fairchild stands almost alone in this tradition. We are lucky to have him."

—Mark Jarman, author of *Bone Fires: New and Selected Poems*

The Blue Buick

The Blue Buick

NEW AND SELECTED POEMS

B. H. FAIRCHILD

 W. W. NORTON & COMPANY   NEW YORK | LONDON

B. H. Fairchild, "The Woman at the Laundromat Crying 'Mercy,'" "The Men," "The Robinson Hotel" (from *Kansas Avenue*), "Flight," "Angels," "Groceries," "Night Shift," "Hair," "To My Friend," "The Limits of My Language," and "Late Game" from *The Arrival of the Future*. Copyright © 2002 by B. H. Fairchild. Reprinted with the permission of The Permissions Company, Inc., on behalf of Alice James Books, www.alicejamesbooks.org.

B. H. Fairchild, "Beauty," "The Invisible Man," "All the People in Hopper's Paintings," "The Book of Hours," "Cigarettes," "The Himalayas," "Body and Soul," "Airlifting Horses," "Old Men Playing Basketball," "Old Woman," "Song," "Thermoregulation in Winter Moths," "Keats," "The Ascension of Ira Campbell," "The Dumka," "A Model of Downtown Los Angeles, 1940," "The Children," "Little Boy," "The Welder, Visited by the Angel of Mercy," "The Death of a Small Town," and "The Art of the Lathe" from *The Art of the Lathe*. Copyright © 1998 by B. H. Fairchild. Reprinted with the permission of The Permissions Company, Inc., on behalf of Alice James Books, www.alicejamesbooks.org.

Excerpts from "The Bridge," from *The Complete Poems of Hart Crane* by Hart Crane, edited by Marc Simon. Copyright 1933, 1958, 1966 by Liveright Publishing Corporation. Copyright © 1986 by Marc Simon. Used by permission of Liveright Publishing Corporation.

For information about permission to reproduce selections from this book, write to Permissions, W. W. Norton & Company, Inc., 500 Fifth Avenue, New York, NY 10110

For information about special discounts for bulk purchases, please contact W. W. Norton Special Sales at specialsales@wwnorton.com or 800-233-4830

Manufacturing by Courier Westford
Book design by Chris Welch
Production manager: Anna Oler

Library of Congress Cataloging-in-Publication Data

Fairchild, B. H.
[Poems. Selections]
The blue buick : new and selected poems / B. H. Fairchild. — First edition.
    pages ; cm
Includes bibliographical references.
ISBN 978-0-393-24026-9 (hardcover)
I. Title.
PS3556.A3625A6 2014
811'.54—dc23

                    2014017290

W. W. Norton & Company, Inc.
500 Fifth Avenue, New York, N.Y. 10110
www.wwnorton.com

W. W. Norton & Company Ltd.
Castle House, 75/76 Wells Street, London W1T 3QT

1 2 3 4 5 6 7 8 9 0

FOR PATRICIA LEA FAIRCHILD,

the air that I breathe

Perhaps they found this front-line trench

at break of day as fully charged as any chorus-end

with hopes and fears; . . . Certainly they sat

curbed, trussed-up, immobile, as men who

consider the Nature of Being.

—DAVID JONES, *In Parenthesis*

CONTENTS

FROM
The Art of the Lathe
(1998)

FROM

Early Occult Memory Systems
of the Lower Midwest
(2003)

FROM
Usher
(2009)

New Poems

FROM

The Arrival of the Future
(1985)

The Woman at the Laundromat Crying "Mercy"

And the glass eyes of dryers whirl
on either side, the roar just loud enough
to still the talk of women. Nothing
is said easily here. Below the screams
of two kids skateboarding in the aisles
thuds and rumbles smother everything,
even the woman crying *mercy, mercy*.

Torn slips of paper on a board swear
Jesus is the Lord, nude photo sessions
can help girls who want to learn, the price
for Sunshine Day School is affordable,
astrology can change your life, any
life. Long white rows of washers lead
straight as highways to a change machine

that turns dollars into dimes to keep
the dryers running. When they stop,
the women lift the dry things out and hold
the sheets between them, pressing corners
warm as babies to their breasts. In back,
the change machine has jammed and a woman
beats it with her fists, crying *mercy, mercy*.

The Men

As a kid sitting in a yellow-vinyl
booth in the back of Earl's Tavern,
you watch the late-afternoon drunks
coming and going, sunlight breaking
through the smoky dark as the door
opens and closes, and it's the future
flashing ahead like the taillights
of a semi as you drop over a rise
in the road on your way to Amarillo,
bright lights and blonde-haired women,
as Billy used to say, slumped over
his beer like a snail, *make a real man*
out of you, the smile bleak as the gaps
between his teeth, *stay loose, son,*
don't die before you're dead. Always
the warnings from men you worked with
before they broke, blue fingernails,
eyes red as fate. *A different life*
for me, you think, and outside later,
feeling young and strong enough to raise
the sun back up, you stare down Highway 54,
pushing everything—stars, sky, moon,
all but a thin line at the edge
of the world—behind you. Your headlights
sweep across the tavern window,
ripping the dark from the small, humped

shapes of men inside who turn and look,
like small animals caught in the glare
of your lights on the road to Amarillo.

The Robinson Hotel

from *Kansas Avenue*, a sequence of five poems

The windows form a sun in white squares.
    Across the street
the Blue Bird Cafe leans into shadow and the cook
    stands in the doorway.
Men from harvest crews step from the Robinson
    in clean white shirts
and new jeans. They stroll beneath the awning,
    smoking Camels,
considering the blue tattoos beneath their sleeves,
    Friday nights
in San Diego years ago, a woman, pink neon lights
    rippling in rainwater.
Tonight, chicken-fried steak and coffee alone
    at the Bluebird,
a double feature at The Plaza: *The Country Girl,*
    The Bridges at Toko-Ri.
The town's night-soul, a marquee flashing orange
    bulbs, stuns the windows
of the Robinson. The men will leave as heroes,
    undiscovered.
Their deaths will be significant and beautiful
    as bright aircraft,
sun glancing on silver wings, twisting, settling
    into green seas.
In their room at night, they see Grace Kelly
    bending at their bedsides.

They move their hands slowly over their chests
    and raise their knees
against the sheets. The Plaza's orange light
    fills the curtains.
Cardboard suitcases lie open, white shirts folded
    like pressed flowers.

Flight

In the early stages of epilepsy there occurs a characteristic
dream. . . . One is somehow lifted free of one's own body;
looking back one sees oneself and feels a sudden,
maddening fear; another presence is entering one's own
person, and there is no avenue of return.

—GEORGE STEINER

Outside my window the wasps
are making their slow circle,
dizzy flights of forage and return,
hovering among azaleas
that bob in a sluggish breeze
this humid, sun-torn morning.

Yesterday my wife held me here
as I thrashed and moaned, her hand
in my foaming mouth, and my son
saw what he was warned he might.

Last night dreams stormed my brain
in thick swirls of shame and fear.
Behind a white garage a locked shed
full of wide-eyed dolls burned,
yellow smoke boiling up in huge clumps
as I watched, feet nailed to the ground.
In dining cars white tablecloths
unfolded wings and flew like gulls.
An old German in a green Homburg
sang lieder, *Mein Herz ist müde.*

In a garden in Pasadena my father
posed in Navy whites while overhead
silver dirigibles moved like great whales.
And in the narrowing tunnel
of the dream's end I flew down
onto the iron red road
of my grandfather's farm.
There was a white rail fence.
In the green meadow beyond,
a small boy walked toward me.
His smile was the moon's rim.
Across his eggshell eyes
ran scenes from my future life,
and he embraced me like a son
or father or my lost brother.

Angels

Elliot Ray Neiderland, home from college
one winter, hauling a load of Herefords
from Hogtown to Guymon with a pint of
Ezra Brooks and a copy of Rilke's *Duineser
Elegien* on the seat beside him, saw the ass-end
of his semi gliding around in the side mirror
as he hit ice and knew he would never live
to see graduation or the castle at Duino.

In the hospital, head wrapped like a gift
(the nurses had stuck a bow on top), he said
four flaming angels crouched on the hood, wings
spread so wide he couldn't see, and then
the world collapsed. We smiled and passed a flask
around. Little Bill and I sang "Your Cheatin'
Heart" and laughed, and then a sudden quiet
put a hard edge on the morning and we left.

Siehe, ich lebe, Look, I'm alive, he said,
leaping down the hospital steps. The nurses
waved, white dresses puffed out like pigeons
in the morning breeze. We roared off in my Dodge,
Behold, I come like a thief! he shouted to the town
and gave his life to poetry. He lives, now,
in the south of France. His poems arrive
by mail, and we read them and do not understand.

Groceries

A woman waits in line and reads
from a book of poems to kill time.

When her items come up to be counted,
the check-out girl greets the book
like a lost child: *The House on Marshland!*

she says, and they share certain lines:
"the late apples, red and gold, / like words
of another language."

The black belt rolls on. Groceries flow,
coagulate, then begin to spill over: canned
corn, chicken pot pies, oatmeal, garden
gloves, apricots, sliced ham, frozen pizza,
loaves and loaves of bread, and then the eggs,

"the sun is shining, everywhere you turn is luck,"
they sing. Here comes the manager, breathless,
eyes like tangerines, hair in flames.

Night Shift

On the down side
of the night shift:
the wind's tense sigh,
the heavy swivel
turning, turning.
Pulling out of the hole
from four thousand feet
straight down,
we change bits, the moon
catching in the old one
a yellow gleam wedged
in mud, a shark's tooth.
The drawworks rumbles
like a flood rushing over
flat stubble fields
that stretch for miles,
all surface, no depth
until now, swept under
ocean, the moon wavering
behind clouds
like a floating body
seen from underwater.
I see small eyes,
feel the hard gray skin
slipping past, and think
of origins, the distances

of time, the absence
of this rig, these men.
On the long drive home
I'll head into a sun
that stared the sea away,
that saw a dried tooth
sink into the darkness
I return to.

Hair

At the 23rd Street Barber Shop
hair is falling across the arms of men,
across white cotton cloths
that drape their bodies like little nightgowns.
How like well-behaved children they seem—
silent, sleepy—sheets tucked
neatly beneath their chins,
legs too short to touch the floor.
Each in his secret life sinks
easily into the fat plastic cushion
and feels the strange lightness of falling hair,
the child's comfort of soft hands
caressing his brow and temples.
Each sighs inwardly to the constant
whisper of scissors about his head,
the razor humming small hymns along his neck.

They've been here a hundred times,
gazed upon mirrors within mirrors,
clusters of slim-necked bottles labeled WILDROOT
and VITALIS, and below the shoeshine stand,
rows of flat gold cans. They've heard
the sudden intimacies, the warmth
of men seduced by grooming: the veteran
confessing an abandoned child in Rome,
men discussing palm-sized pistols,

small enough to snuggle against your stomach.
As children they were told, after you're dead
it keeps on growing, and they've seen themselves
lying in hair long as a young girl's.

Two of them rise and walk slowly out.
Their round heads blaze in the doorway.
They creep into what is left of day, fingertips
touching the short, stiff hairs across their necks.

To My Friend

To my friend they all look like movie stars.
"Here comes Herbert Lom," he'll say, and a guy
in a low-angle shot looms over us, bulging
forehead shouting *treason* to pedestrians.
This history of personalities repeats itself each day.
"Take a look at ZaSu Pitts behind the pineapples"
or "Jesus, Zachary Scott sacking groceries!"
He collects them like old stills, hunts for them
in every bar, smoke-curls and clicking glasses
whispering sly promises of Sidney Greenstreet.
Or at traffic lights: Ginger Rogers in a Dodge,
Errol Flynn on a blue Suzuki. The glamour
of appearances. The way montage erases vast
ontological gaps. A wino as Quasimodo as Anthony
Quinn explains the brunette cheerleader, who is
really Gina Lollobrigida. Life connects this way,
but huge sympathies are lost in a single shot.
Sitting here in the Knox Street Tavern, I see what
he means: the inevitable crowd scene, brick street
lifted into light, flat faces rounding into possibility.
Behind the bar Eric von Stroheim smokes a Gauloise,
merciless and cool, contemplating so many frames
per second, the small darknesses we never see.

The Limits of My Language: English 85B

The black shawl falls from your shoulders
as you rise against your daughter's tugs
and whispers, and your withered mouth
opens in a dry quaver like voices
heard across a windblown field, *Rock of Ages,*
cleft for me, and my students wake to listen.

On that first day she whispered, warning me:
She thinks she's in church. She's my mother
and I'll have to bring her every day.
Your eyes wandered like fish behind a glass
and your crooked hand jerked back from mine.

So I've become a minister to you,
some fundamental backwoods screamer,
redeemer of Oklahoma souls, surrounded
by a choir of distant kinfolk robed
in flecks of stained-glass light and shade.
"The Old Rugged Cross" or "Bringing in the Sheaves"
lifts you right out of your seat at times,
and we wait while your daughter puts you
back in place: *Be quiet now, Momma.*

There's no time for that. In her voice
I hear your own among hymns hovering
on an Oklahoma Sunday years ago
inside a white frame church *let me hide*
myself in thee and in your shaken glance
and palsied hands I see you kneeling there
beneath dim memories of burnt-out fields
and black locust clouds looming down
wailing with God's own sorrow *let the water*
and the blood creek floods crawling
across gray moonlit ground, black hours
in storm cellars between dank earth walls
from thy riven side which flowed your mother
crying, the same hymns hanging in the air
like dust as you knelt there that Sunday,
clump of cinquefoil in your fist, big ribboned
Easter hat pulled back, as the preacher man
laid hands on you and promised everything:
hope, happiness, the heaven of eternal Being.

And so, through a dustbowl girlhood, a husband
headed for hell, and one daughter who turned out
right, you saved your best for last. Now
you come into my room and take your place
and stare into some space beyond these walls.
Every time I take a stick of chalk,

you see the wafer in my hand.
Every time I write a word across the board,
you see me beckon to the choir.
Every time I ask is this a verb or noun,
you turn the pages of your book.
And when I spread my arms for answers,
you rise slowly to sing, *Amazing grace,*
how sweet the sound, out of time and place.

Late Game

for Paul

If this is soccer,
the moon's up for grabs.

It floats low over the goalee,
whose father waits downfield
measuring the distance,
several white lines
that flame then fade
like breaking waves.

The players pull night
behind them.
Luminous uniforms
move the white ball
quietly here, there.

Then out of these blurred
frail bodies
the ball looms.

His son's arms flash
against the moon,
catching it,

and one pale cry leaps
toward the stars.

FROM

Local Knowledge

(1991)

In Czechoslovakia

It is 1968, and you are watching a movie
called *The Shop on Main Street,* about a man—
an ordinary man, a carpenter—in Czechoslovakia,
who is appointed Aryan Controller of a poor button shop
belonging to the widow Lautmannová, who is old
and deaf and has the eyes of a feverish child.
She smiles in luminous gratitude for almost anything—
the empty button boxes, a photo of her lost daughters,
the man, Tóno, who she believes has come to help her.

At the point where the two meet—she, kind but confused,
he, awkward and somewhat ashamed—you notice a woman
in the front row who keeps bending toward the seat
beside her and whispering and letting her hand drift
lovingly toward whomever—a child, you suppose—is there.
The woman's frizzy hair catches the reflected light
from the screen, a nimbus of fire around her head
as she turns to share her popcorn with the child whose
fine blonde hair and green eyes you have begun to imagine.

In the movie Tóno has failed to explain his position
to the widow and is acting as her helper in exchange
for monthly payments from the Jewish community.
He is contented, his ambitious wife is enjoying
dreams of prosperity and a heightened sexuality,
it is that terrible time when everyone is happier
than they should be, and then of course the trucks

move in, the dependable gray trucks that have made
life somewhat impossible in the twentieth century.

Now the woman in the front row has returned
to her seat and is handing a Coke to the child
hidden by the chair back, then reaching over
with a handkerchief to wipe the child's mouth
and smile and whisper out of that explosion of hair
she wears. The widow Lautmannová cannot understand
the trucks or Tóno's dilemma that either she must go
or he will be arrested as a collaborator, and as he
stands there pleading, going crazy in her husband's suit

which she has given to him, her eyes widen
like opened fists and she knows now and begins
to shout, *pogrom, pogrom,* with her hands trembling
like moths around her face, and when he panics
and hurls her into the closet to hide her, she falls
and oh Jesus he has killed her and he cries out,
I am a zero, but you think, no, no, it's worse,
you're a man, and now the woman in the front row
is shouting at the child, it's misbehaved in some way,

and when you look up my God Tóno has hung himself
in the suit that belonged to the widow's husband,
the suit he was married in, and then, miraculously,

Tóno and the widow are floating arm in arm,
smiling, dancing out into the sun-drenched boulevard,
dancing away from you and history, resurrected
into the world as it might be but somehow cannot be,
a grove of light where the cobbled streets and trees
with their wire skirts are glossy after a soft rain

and the world deepens without darkening and the faces
of everyone are a kind of ovation, and then it's over,
you think, the house lights go up, and you're sitting there
stunned and the woman from the front row walks out
into the aisle with her hand out behind her as if gripping
another, smaller hand. And you see it, though
you don't want to, because you are a man or a woman,
you see that there is nothing there, no child,
nothing, and the woman stops and bends down to speak

to the child that isn't there and she has this smile
of adoration, this lacemaker's gaze of contentment,
she is perfectly happy, and she walks on out
into the street where people are walking up and down
and where you will have to walk up and down
as if you were on a boulevard in Czechoslovakia
watching that endless cortege of gray trucks
rumble by in splendid alignment as you go on thinking
and breathing as usual, wreathed in your own human skin.

In a Café near Tuba City, Arizona, Beating My Head against a Cigarette Machine

> . . . the sea shall give up her dead; and the corruptible bodies of
> those who sleep in him shall be changed, and made like unto
> his glorious body.
>
> —BOOK OF COMMON PRAYER

The ruptured Pontiac, comatose and tilted on three wheels,
seems to sink slowly like a drunken ship into the asphalt.
My wife wanders aimlessly further into despair and an absence
of traffic, waving invisible semaphores along the embankment.
The infant we have misnamed after a suicidal poet writhes
in harness across my back, her warm urine funneling between
my buttocks, and her yowls rip like sharks through the gray heat.
But still beyond the screams I hear somehow the flutter
of chicken wings, buckets rattling, the howl of spaniels,
and my grandfather's curse grinding against the dull, unjust sky
of God and Oklahoma. I have given the waitress all my money,
and she has taken it, stuffed it into the heart-shaped pocket stamped
with her ridiculous name, and removed herself to the storeroom
with the cook who wants only to doze through the afternoon lull
undisturbed by a man who has yanked the PALL MALL knob
from the cigarette machine and now beats his head against
the coin return button while mumbling the prayer for the Burial
of the Dead at Sea which his grandmother taught him as a charm
against drowning in the long silences before tornadoes
and floods when Black Bear Creek rose on the Otoe
and the windmill began to shriek like a gang of vampires.
In the shards of the machine's mirror I see the black line

of blood dividing my forehead and a dozen versions of my wife
sobbing now at the screen door while behind her our laundry
has flown free of the Pontiac's wired trunk lid and drifts
like gulls across the vast sea, the difficult sea surrounding
Tuba City, Arizona, and my grandparents walk slowly
toward us over the water in the serene and noble attitude of gods.

Language, Nonsense, Desire

Professor Ramirez dozes behind the projector,
Conversación Español lapping over the bored
shoulders of sophomores who dissolve in the film's
languor of talk and coffee at a sidewalk café
in Madrid or Barcelona or some other luminous
Mediterranean dream. The tanned faces rounding
into the Spanish air like bowls of still-life fruit
offer little dialogues about streetcars or feathers
over a clutter of plates and delicate white cups
of mocha blend. The hands of the speakers
are bright birds that lift and tremble among
the anomalies of ordinary life: *piñatas,* cousins
who live in Peru, the last train to Zaragoza.
The speakers are three friends forever entangled
in the syntax of Spanish 101, fated to shape
loose chatter into harmonies of discourse, arias
of locus, *¿Dónde está la casa?* and possession,
Yo tengo un perro: Raoul, his dark, hungry
profile immaculately defined against the pallor
of a white beach; the housewife Esmeralda erotic
in her onyx curls, recalling a Catholic childhood,
that same black extravagance pressed against
her pillow as she listened to the nun read stories
and imagined herself as a gaucho, drunk and love-
crazed in the hills of Argentina; and wan Julio,
articulate, epicene, fluttering his pianist's fingers

as he croons melodiously about the rush of time:
¿Qué hora es? ¿Son las dos? ¡Ay! And always
in the background along the periphery of syllable
and gesture, the silent pilgrimage of traffic
and commerce and light-dazzled crowds with some
destination, some far blue promise to carry them
through the day, some end to speech and love.

There Is Constant Movement in My Head

The choreographer from Nebraska
is listening to her mother's cane
hammering the dance floor, down, down,
like some gaunt, rapacious bird
digging at a rotted limb. The mother
still beats time in her daughter's head.

There is constant movement in my head,
the choreographer begins. In Nebraska
I learned dance and guilt from my mother,
held my hands out straight until the cane
beat my palms blue. I was a wild bird
crashing into walls, calming down

only to dance. When Tallchief came down
from New York, a dream flew into my head:
to be six feet tall, to dance *The Firebird*
all in black and red, to shock Nebraska
with my naked, crazy leaps until the cane
shook in the furious hand of my mother.

Well, that day never came. My mother
thought I could be whittled down,
an oak stump to carve into some cane
she could lean on. But in my head

were the sandhill cranes that crossed Nebraska
each fall: sluggish, great-winged birds

lumbering from our pond, the air bird-
heavy with cries and thrumming. My mother
knew. She said I would leave Nebraska,
that small-town life could only pull me down.
Then her hands flew up around her head
and she hacked at the air with her cane.

There are movements I can't forget: the cane
banging the floor, dancers like huge birds
struggling into flight, and overhead,
the choreography of silver cranes my mother
always watched when the wind blew down
from the sandhills and leaves fell on Nebraska.

This dance is the cane of my mother.
The dancers are birds that will never come down.
They were all in my head when I left Nebraska.

Maize

After Roland Stills fell from the top of the GANO
grain elevator, we felt obliged in some confused,
floundering way as if his hand had just pulled
the red flag from our pockets and we had turned
to find not him but rows of Kansas maize
reeling into the sun, we felt driven to recall
more than perhaps, drunk, we saw: trees squatting
below like pond frogs, mare's tails sweeping the hills,
and the moon in its floppy dress riding low behind
the shock of his yellow hair as, falling, he seemed
to drop to his knees, drunk, passing out, *oh shit,*
with the same stupid grin as when he might recite
Baudelaire in the company of a girl and a small glass
of Cointreau, *Je suis comme le roi d'un pays pluvieux.*
And beyond his eyes blooming suddenly into white
flowers were the lights of houses where our parents
spoke of harvest like a huge wall they would climb
to come again to a new life. Driving along dirt roads
in our trucks, we would look through the scrim of dust
at the throbbing land and rows of red maize whipping past
before the hard heat of summer when the combines
came pushing their shadows and shouldering each other
dark as clouds erasing the horizon, coming down
on the fields to cut the maize, to cut it down
in a country without rain or the grace of kings.

In Another Life I Encounter My Father

There we are in the same outfield,
a minor league team named after some small
but ferocious animal—the Badgers, say,
or Bulldogs. The town is heavily industrial,
Peoria maybe, and the slap of the fungo bat
keeps us moving over the worn grass—in,
then back, where a blonde drinking a beer
is painted crudely on a white fence.
Big drops of condensation drape the bottle,
which is angled toward her open mouth.
We want to joke about this, but don't.
He is new on the team, and we are uneasy
with each other. When a high one drifts
far to his right, he takes it on a dead run.
He is more graceful than I am, and faster.

In the dugout he offers me a chew,
and we begin to talk—hometown, college ball,
stuff like that. A copy of Rimbaud
sticks out of my pocket, and I give him
the line about *begging the day for mercy.*
He frowns, spitting, working his glove.
We begin to talk politics, baseball
as ideology, more embracing than Marxism.
He seems interested, but something is wrong.
The sky is getting a yellow tinge.

The heavy air droops over my shoulders,
and the locusts begin their harangue.
When I go to the plate, the ball
floats by fat as a cantaloupe, and I
slam it through the left field lights.

I can do no wrong, but we are losing.
The coach, an alcoholic, is beginning
to cry over his second wife. His wails
unnerve us. The catcher is stoned,
and we may have to forfeit. The new guy
is unperturbed and praises me lavishly
on my fine play. In the outfield I point out
Draco and Cassiopeia, almost missing one
that drives me into the fence. I hold
the ball high and tip my cap, the crowd
roars, blood runs down my back. Walking in,
he knows I am playing over my head, but says
nothing. We hear the batboy's shriek,
the coach's tired moan. The locusts
are shredding the air like band saws,
the scoreboard is blazing at the edges,
and we know that the game will never end.

The Machinist, Teaching His Daughter to Play the Piano

The brown wrist and hand with its raw knuckles and blue nails
      packed with dirt and oil, pause in midair,
the fingers arched delicately,

and she mimics him, hand held just so, the wrist loose,
      then swooping down to the wrong chord.
She lifts her hand and tries again.

Drill collars rumble, hammering the nubbin-posts.
      The helper lifts one, turning it slowly,
then lugs it into the lathe's chuck.

The bit sheers the dull iron into new metal, falling
      into the steady chant of lathework,
and the machinist lights a cigarette, holding

in his upturned palms the polonaise he learned at ten,
      then later the easiest waltzes,
études, impossible counterpoint

like the voice of his daughter he overhears one night
      standing in the backyard. She is speaking
to herself but not herself, as in prayer,

the listener is some version of herself
      and the names are pronounced carefully,
self-consciously: Chopin, Mozart,

Scarlatti . . . these gestures of voice and hands
        suspended over the keyboard
that move like the lathe in its turning

toward music, the wind dragging the hoist chain, the ring
        of iron on iron in the holding rack.
His daughter speaks to him one night,

but not to him, rather someone created between them,
        a listener, there and not there,
a master of lathes, a student of music.

The Doppler Effect

When I would go into bars in those days,
the hard round faces would turn
to speak something like loneliness
but deeper, the rain spilling into gutters
or the sound of a car pulling away
in a moment of sleeplessness just before dawn,
the Doppler effect, I would have said shrewdly then,
of faces diminishing slightly into the distance
even as they spoke. Their children
were doing well, somewhere, and their wives
were somewhere, too, and we were here
with those bright euphoric flowers
unfolding slowly in our eyes
and the sun which we had not seen for days
nuzzling our fingertips and licking
our elbows. Oh, it was all there,
and there again the same, our heads nodding,
hands resting lightly upon the mahogany sheen
of the bar. Then someone would leave
and the door would turn to a yellow square
so sudden and full of fire
that our eyes would daze and we would
stare into the long mirrors for hours
and speak shrewdly of that pulling away,
that going toward something.

Toban's Precision Machine Shop

It has just rained, a slow movement of Mahler
drifts from Toban's office in back, the windows
blurred by runnels of oil and dirt, and I walk
into the grease-and-water smell like a child
entering his grandfather's closet. It is a shop
so old the lathes are driven by leather belts
looping down like enormous hackamores
from a long shaft beneath the tin roof's peak.

Such emptiness. Such a large and palpable
sculpture of disuse: lathes leaning against
their leather straps, grinding wheels motionless
above mounds of iron filings. Tools lie lead-
heavy along the backs of steel workbenches,
burnished where the morning light leaks through
and lifts them up. Calipers and honing cloths
hang suspended in someone's dream of perfection.

There are times when the sun lingers over
the green plastic panels on the roof, and light
seems to rise from the floor, seems to lift lathes
and floor at once, and something announces itself,
not beauty, but rather its possibility,
and you almost reach out, almost lean forward
to lie down in that wash of bronze light, as if
it would bear you up, would hold you in sleep.

Toban no longer sees the shop advancing
into its day's purchase of light and dark.
He sits in his office among his books
with music settling down on his shoulders
like a warm shawl. He replaces the Mahler
with Schubert, the B-flat sonata, and sends it
unraveling toward me, turning the sound
far above the cluttered silence of the lathes.

Speaking the Names

When frost first enters the air
in the country of moon and stars,
the world has glass edges, and the hard glint
of crystals seeping over iron
makes even the abandoned tractor seem all night sky and starlight.

On the backporch taking deep breaths like some miracle cure,
breathe, let the spirit move you,
here I am after the long line of cigarettes
that follows grief like a curse, trying to breathe, revive,
in this land of revivals and lost farms . . .

It is no good to grow up hating the rich.
In spring I would lie down among pale anemone and primrose
and listen to the river's darkening hymn, and soon
the clouds were unraveling like the frayed sleeves of field hands,
and ideology had flown with the sparrows.

The cottonwood that sheltered the henhouse is a stump now,
and the hackberries on the north were leveled years ago.
Bluestem hides the cellar, with its sweet gloom of clay walls and bottles.
The silo looms over the barn, whose huge door swallowed daylight,
where a child could enter his own death.

What became of the boy with nine fingers?
The midwife from Yellow Horse who raised geese?

They turned their backs on the hard life,
and from the tree line along the river they seem to rise now,
her plain dress bronze in moonlight, his wheatshock hair in flames.

Behind me is a house without people. And so, for my sake
I bring them back, watching the quick cloud of vapor that blooms
and vanishes with each syllable: *O.T.* and *Nellie Swearingen,*
their children, *Locie, Dorrel, Deanie, Bill,*
and the late *Vinna Adams,* whose name I speak into the bright and final air.

Local Knowledge

It seems hard to find an acceptable answer to the question
of how or why the world conceives a desire, and discovers
an ability, to see itself, and appears to suffer the process.
That it does so is sometimes called the original mystery.

—G. SPENCER BROWN, *LAWS OF FORM*

I.

A rusted-out Ford Fairlane with red star hubcaps
skids up to Neiderland Rig Local No. 1
heaving Travis Deeds into a swirl of dust
and rainbowed pools of oil and yellow mud.

Rows of drill collars stand in racks and howl
in the blunt wind. Chain and hoist cable
bang the side of a tin bunkhouse as men stunned
with hangovers wake to the drum of a new day.

Crowding around the rig floor where the long
column of iron reaches straight down through rock
and salt water, Travis and the men grab
the big tongs and throw them on, then off,

hauling up one length of pipe, then another
as the bit drags out of the hole, coming up
with crushed rock and shark's teeth from old strata
once under ocean. The drawworks lurches, rumbling

loud enough to smother talk, and the men
work under the iron brand of the noon sun
until mud covers them. Their arms and faces
blacken, and gas fumes sting their eyes.

Two hundred feet up, the crown block pulleys
wail on their axles like high wires, keening.
Travis leans back to see the black mud-hose curl
into a question mark looming from earth to sun.

II.

Dear Father,
*   As you can see I have*
come pretty far north with this bunch
almost to Amarillo in a stretch
of wheat field flat and blowed out as any

to be seen in West Texas. All things
are full of weariness, as the man says,
and I am one of those things, dog-tired
and not fit to shoot. I am very glad

to hear you are back with your church
in Odessa if that is what you want

and if that old bottle does not bring
you down again though it is a comfort

to me, which you do not want to hear,
but alone up there in the crow's nest
with the wind screaming at me
and that old devil moon staring down

and nothing all around, you get to thinking
you are pretty much nothing yourself.
But I am all OK, staying out
of trouble, and I do not know where

I am going in this world but am looking
as always for a fat paycheck and then
I will be home again. Take good care
of yourself.
                    Your loving son,
                            Travis

III.

Travis Deeds's tongue, throat, wide mouth:
singers of broken tunes and his father's hymns

in dry creek beds alone with Jack Daniel's
and the arc of night, the revolving stars.

The eyes pink from booze, dust, and sunlight,
sleepless beneath a football scar that slices
the left eyebrow like a scythe, readers
of Job and Ecclesiastes, crazed in moonlight.

Belly, back, shoulders pale as eggs,
once-broken arm bent slightly, hands mottled
with scraped knuckles and blue fingernails
that thrum like drumfish with the blood's pulse.

Birthmark like a splash of acid on one thigh,
darkening hair of the loins, sad cock, legs thick
as stumps, knees yellow-brown with old bruises,
ludicrous feet, small toes curled like snails.

Slowly the traveling block lifts his body
to the rig's top. Blond hair blazing, he sings
flat against the hard wind, rising, staring down
into the rig's black strata, the fossil kingdom.

IV.

Dearest son,
          What gain has the worker
from his toil? *I'm a little short here,*
and if you could spare maybe fifty?
Am back on my feet, though, feisty

and full of the Word. So I turned
to consider wisdom and madness
and folly, *and so should you for one*
of these days God will show His face

to you as He has to me, you think
your alone in this world, that your
nothing, but you are not, believe me.
There is more to life than sweat

and dirt and oil and fat paychecks.
Remember, better is a handful
of quietness than two hands full
of toil and a striving after wind.

I know this in my poor banged-up soul
I hope you can come home soon

for it is lonely as hell here, that old wolf
scratching at my door.

Love,

Avon

V.

Gargantuan plates move over the mantle of the earth.
The jammed crust up-thrusts and rivers spill down,
dumping red dirt in layers, choking themselves dry.
On the west, the Pecos River; on the east,

canyons of the high plains: Palo Duro,
Tule, Casa Blanca, Quitaque, Yellow House.
Calcium bubbles up to form the caprock.
Sod grass spreads under the wind. The dirt holds.

Around the rig now, plowed fields lose the dirt
in gusts, and roughnecks breathe through rags
like small-time bandits. Five miles east, a gray wolf
drags its kill beneath a jagged branch of mesquite.

Under the raucous sky sandhill cranes ruffle
the pond water with their wings, lumbering into flight.

Everywhere the flat land has given up its wheat
and maize, and dust rises along the horizon

like a huge planet out of orbit, colliding.
Travis Deeds, greasing the crown block,
leans against the wind and sees the open mouth
of the sun slowly drowning in the brown air.

VI.

Dear Father,
Enclosed is a check
for fifty bucks, please hang onto it.
Good news here. The geologist took
what is called a core sample and says

that it is a sure thing this time.
As for your letter, you say not
to feel like nothing, but it seems to me
there is a lot to be said for nothing.

The other night I was alone
with just the moon and stars
and the locusts buzzing away
and could look down the hole

into the nothing of the earth
and above into the nothing of the sky
and there I was in the middle
of it all until I was nothing too

not even Travis Deeds but just the eye
that the world uses to look at itself.
So maybe that is a place in the world,
not that you would agree. But I am

on day shift now and if the geologist
is right and we are right next door
to pay dirt, I should be home soon
with my sack full.
                    Your loving son,
                        Travis

        VII.

Crew, drawworks, the whole rig floor are dragged
under the dirt storm, roughneck shouts sinking
beneath the wind's harangue, the berserk clatter
of chains, cable, bunkhouse roof yanking loose.

And for a while in the sudden rush and whirl
the body clings to the crown block, grease-slick
hands grasping, then spilling like fish over
the iron rails as the false night swallows

the land the way the land folds its creatures
into bedrock fossils. The body is blown free.
The arms wheel, the legs blunder like tossed sticks,
the soft earth surrounds and pulls him down.

Blood batters the heart in flight, pounding
like the flailing wings of cranes, the quickening
breath of the wolf returning to his kill,
the mesquite branch shaking in the nervous wind.

Put forth thy hand now and touch his bone and flesh.
And the men gather where he slams the ground,
where the body is the obedient son of gravity,
where his hands claw the thickening dust, where

the buckled spine rages, where the unknowable God
does not speak the unknowable answer and the great wing
folds and unfolds and once more under the sun's
long pull the wind makes its hollow yowl of lament.

Kansas

Leaning against my car after changing the oil,
I hold my black hands out and stare into them
as if they were the faces of my children looking
at the winter moon and thinking of the snow
that will erase everything before they wake.

In the garage, my wife comes behind me
and slides her hands beneath my soiled shirt.
Pressing her face between my shoulder blades,
she mumbles something, and soon we are laughing,
wrestling like children among piles of old rags,

towels that unravel endlessly, torn sheets,
work shirts from twenty years ago when I stood
in the door of a machine shop, grease-blackened,
and Kansas lay before me blazing with new snow,
a future of flat land, white skies, and sunlight.

After making love, we lie on the abandoned
mattress and stare at our pale winter bodies
sprawling in the half-light. She touches her belly,
the scar of our last child, and the black
prints of my hands along her hips and thighs.

The Soliloquy of the Appliance Repairman

They bring me their broken toasters,
chrome-dulled and shorted on lumps of grease,
twisted Mixmasters with mangled blades
and bent spindles punch-drunk
and beaten into an early grave.
And I, healer and name-brand magician,
I must raise them from the dead,
prop them up and coax their failed motors
into the life signs of hum and whir.

They go out, they come back,
these wounded, cracked plastic-and-chrome marvels
of the mediocre, of the watery omelette
and bland, confused margarita.
We should learn from our mistakes:
the lawnmower plugged with muddy oil
will foul again, and again
the nightmare ice maker will vomit
its perfectly formed cubes into the void.
Freon again and oh ever again freon
spewing through the endless circuitry of the freezer,
thumping along, hissing through leaks.

The two girls who lugged in
the computerized cappuccino machine,
chattering and letting their bright eyes

and flashing hands erase the shadows
of the shop—how could they have known my limits:
the modern and high-tech, the microwave ovens,
for instance, with their digital readouts
and soft little gongs that puzzled me
almost into retirement months ago.
Give it up, my wife said,
you're as obsolete as they are,
pointing to the prewar junk piling up unclaimed.

The girls frowned and took it back.
Hunching their shoulders like old women,
they stumbled out, letting the door bang shut,
flinging the shop back into darkness.
I have learned from the inventions of history,
but I live in the age of wonders,
of the self-contained and irreparable,
where I stand and watch
the small, good things of my hands
drifting far away into the corners of my life.

Work

Work is a transient form of mechanical energy by means
of which certain transformations of other forms of energy
are brought about through the agency of a force acting through
a distance. . . . Work done by lifting a body stores mechanical
potential energy in the system consisting of the body and the
earth. Work done on a body to set it in motion stores mechanical
kinetic energy in the system of which the body is one part.

—*HANDBOOK OF ENGINEERING FUNDAMENTALS*

I. Work

Drill collars lie on racks and howl
in the blunt wind. A winch truck waits
in the shop yard beside an iron block,
hook and cable coiling down, dragging
through dirt that blows in yellow gusts.

East across a field where the slag sky
of morning bends down, a man walks away
from a white frame house and a woman
who shouts and waves from the back porch.
He can hear the shop doors banging open.

Inside, where the gray light lifts dust
in swirls, tools rest like bodies dull
with sleep. The lathe shudders and
starts its dark groan, the chuck's jaw
gripping an iron round, the bit set.

Outside, the man approaches the iron block,
a rotary table, judging its weight,
the jerk and pull on the hoist chain.
A bad sun heaves the shadow of his house
outward. He bends down. A day begins.

II. The Body

Looping the chain through the block's eyes,
he makes a knot and pulls the cable hook through.
The winch motor starts up, reeling in cable slowly

until it tightens, then drops to a lower gear
and begins to lift. The motor's whine brings
machinists to the shop windows, sends sparrows

fluttering from highwires where the plains wind
gives its bleak moan and sigh. When the brake
is thrown, the block jerks and sways five feet

above the earth, straining to return, popping
a loose cable thread and making the gin poles
screech in their sockets like grief-stricken women.

From the house the man is lost in the blaze of a sun
gorged to bursting and mirrored in the shop's
tin side. The block hangs, black in the red air.

III. The Body and the Earth

Beneath the rotary table the man reaches up
to remove the huge bearings, and oil winds
like a rope down his arm. He places
each bearing big as a pendulum in the sun

where it shines, swathed in grease.
It is the heart of the day, and he feels
the sudden breeze cool his face and forearms,
wet now with the good sweat of hard work.

The wind scrapes through stubble, making
a papery sound that reminds him of harvest:
him, his father, the field hands crowded around
a beer keg to celebrate the week's cut, dirt

drying to mud on their damp faces, leaving
bruises and black masks. Now, kneeling
in the block's cool shadow, he watches clods
soak up the brown pools of oil and sweat.

IV. The System of Which the Body Is One Part

On the downside of the workday,
when the wind shifts and heat stuns the ground
like an iron brand, the machinists lean
into the shadow of the shop's eaves
and gulp ice water, watching the yard hand now

as he struggles in his black square
to slip each bearing back in place, each steel ball
that mirrors back his eyes, the stubble field, the shop,
the white frame house, the sun, and everything beyond,
the whole circumference of seen and unseen, the world

stretching away in its one last moment
when the chain makes that odd grunting noise,
and sighs *click,* and then *click,* and sings through the eyes
of the block as it slams the ground and the earth takes
the thud and the men freeze and the woman strolls out to see
what has happened now in the system of which the body is one part.

L'Attente

The little man sitting at the top of the stairs
looked up at me through eyes dark and unreachable
as stones at the bottom of a pond, and said,
Waiting is the brother of death.

In Degas' painting, a woman dressed
in the native costume of death waits
seated on a bench beside her daughter,
a ballerina in blue ribbons and white
crinoline who is bent over slightly
as if she might be ill, ill with waiting,
the harness of the future heavy
around her neck. The mother leans forward,
elbows resting on thighs, and holds
her umbrella out before her in a kind
of resignation, a dropped semaphore,
a broken code. She is beyond language,
and though you cannot see her eyes
beneath the wide brim of her black hat,
something about the jaw and chin, some
thin line of shadow, tells you the eyes
are set in the dazed stare of memory,
the white gloves she wears are the white dresses
of childhood, the white Sunday mornings
narrowing toward the vanishing point
like rows of sycamore along the boulevard.

I said to the little man at the top
of the stairs, *Yes, I know, I am waiting, too.*
And I invited him in for a cup of tea.
Then we sat down at the table on the balcony
drinking our tea, not speaking, warm
in each other's company, like children
waiting for a ballet class to begin,
waiting for the dancing to begin.

The Art of the Lathe
(1998)

Beauty

Therefore,
Their sons grow suicidally beautiful . . .

—JAMES WRIGHT,
"AUTUMN BEGINS IN MARTIN'S FERRY, OHIO"

I.

We are at the Bargello in Florence, and she says,
what are you thinking? And I say, *beauty,* thinking
of how very far we are now from the machine shop
and the dry fields of Kansas, the treeless horizons
of slate skies and the muted passions of roughnecks
and scrabble farmers drunk and romantic enough
to weep more or less silently at the darkened end
of the bar out of, what else, loneliness, meaning
the ache of thwarted desire, of, in a word, *beauty,*
or rather its absence, and it occurs to me again
that no male member of my family has ever used
this word in my hearing or anyone else's except
in reference, perhaps, to a new pickup or dead deer.
This insight, this backward vision, first came to me
as a young man as some weirdness of the air waves
slipped through the static of our new Motorola
with a discussion of *beauty* between Robert Penn Warren
and Paul Weiss at Yale College. We were in Kansas
eating barbecue-flavored potato chips and waiting
for *Father Knows Best* to float up through the snow
of rural TV in 1963. I felt transported, stunned.

Here were two grown men discussing "beauty"
seriously and with dignity as if they and the topic
were as normal as normal topics of discussion
between men such as soybean prices or why
the commodities market was a sucker's game
or Oklahoma football or Gimpy Neiderland
almost dying from his hemorrhoid operation.
They were discussing beauty and tossing around
allusions to Plato and Aristotle and someone
named Pater, and they might be homosexuals.
That would be a natural conclusion, of course,
since here were two grown men talking about "beauty"
instead of scratching their crotches and cursing
the goddamned government trying to run everybody's
business. Not a beautiful thing, that. The government.
Not beautiful, though a man would not use that word.
One time my Uncle Ross from California called my mom's
Sunday dinner centerpiece "lovely," and my father
left the room, clearly troubled by the word *lovely*
coupled probably with the very idea of California
and the fact that my Uncle Ross liked to tap-dance.
The light from the venetian blinds, the autumn,
silver Kansas light laving the table that Sunday,
is what I recall now because it was beautiful,
though I of course would not have said so then, *beautiful,*
as so many moments forgotten but later remembered

come back to us in slants and pools and uprisings of light,
beautiful in itself, but more beautiful mingled
with memory, the light leaning across my mother's
carefully set table, across the empty chair
beside my Uncle Ross, the light filtering down
from the green plastic slats in the roof of the machine shop
where I worked with my father so many afternoons,
standing or crouched in pools of light and sweat with men
who knew the true meaning of labor and money and other
hard, true things and did not, did not ever, use the word, *beauty*.

II.

Late November, shadows gather in the shop's north end,
and I'm watching Bobby Sudduth do piecework on the Hobbs.
He fouls another cut, *motherfucker, fucking bitch machine,*
and starts over, sloppy, slow, about two joints away
from being fired, but he just doesn't give a shit.
He sets the bit again, white wrists flashing in the lamplight
and showing botched, blurred tattoos, both from a night
in Tijuana, and continues his sexual autobiography,
that's right, fucked my own sister, and I'll tell you, bud,
it wasn't bad. Later, in the Philippines, the clap:
as far as I'm concerned, any man who hasn't had VD
just isn't a man. I walk away, knowing I have just heard

the dumbest remark ever uttered by man or animal.
The air around me hums in a dark metallic bass,
light spilling like grails of milk as someone opens
the mammoth shop door. A shrill, sullen truculence
blows in like dust devils, the hot wind nagging
my blousy overalls, and in the sideyard the winch truck
backfires and stalls. The sky yellows. Barn sparrows cry
in the rafters. That afternoon in Dallas Kennedy is shot.

Two weeks later sitting around on rotary tables
and traveling blocks whose bearings litter the shop floor
like huge eggs, we close our lunch boxes and lean back
with cigarettes and watch smoke and dust motes rise and drift
into sunlight. All of us have seen the newscasts,
photographs from *Life,* have sat there in our cavernous rooms,
assassinations and crowds flickering over our faces,
some of us have even dreamed it, sleeping through
the TV's drone and flutter, seen her arm reaching
across the lank body, black suits rushing in like moths,
and the long snake of the motorcade come to rest,
then the announcer's voice as we wake astonished in the dark.
We think of it now, staring at the tin ceiling like a giant screen,
what a strange goddamned country, as Bobby Sudduth
arches a wadded Fritos bag at the time clock and says,
Oswald, from that far, you got to admit, that shot was a beauty.

III.

The following summer. A black Corvette gleams like a slice
of onyx in the sideyard, driven there by two young men
who look like Marlon Brando and mention Hollywood
when Bobby asks where they're from. The foreman, my father,
has hired them because we're backed up with work, both shop
and yard strewn with rig parts, flat-bed haulers rumbling
in each day lugging damaged drawworks, and we are desperate.
The noise is awful, a gang of roughnecks from a rig
on down-time shouting orders, our floor hands knee-deep
in the drawwork's gears heating the frozen sleeves and bushings
with cutting torches until they can be hammered loose.
The iron shell bangs back like a drumhead. Looking
for some peace, I walk onto the pipe rack for a quick smoke,
and this is the way it begins for me, this memory,
this strangest of all memories of the shop and the men
who worked there, because the silence has come upon me
like the shadow of cranes flying overhead as they would
each autumn, like the quiet and imperceptible turning
of a season, the shop has grown suddenly still here
in the middle of the workday, and I turn to look
through the tall doors where the machinists stand now
with their backs to me, the lathes whining down together,
and in the shop's center I see them standing in a square

of light, the two men from California, as the welders
lift their black masks, looking up, and I see their faces first,
the expressions of children at a zoo, perhaps,
or after a first snow, as the two men stand naked,
their clothes in little piles on the floor as if they
are about to go swimming, and I recall how fragile
and pale their bodies seemed against the iron and steel
of the drill presses and milling machines and lathes.
I did not know the word, *exhibitionist,* then, and so
for a moment it seemed only a problem of memory,
that they had *forgotten* somehow where they were,
that this was not the locker room after the game,
that they were not taking a shower, that this was not
the appropriate place, and they would then remember,
and suddenly embarrassed, begin shyly to dress again.
But they did not, and in memory they stand frozen
and poised as two models in a drawing class,
of whom the finished sketch might be said, though not by me
nor any man I knew, to be beautiful, they stand there
forever, with the time clock ticking behind them,
time running on but not moving, like the white tunnel
of silence between the snap of the ball and the thunderclap
of shoulder pads that never seems to come and then
there it is, and I hear a quick intake of breath
on my right behind the Hobbs and it is Bobby Sudduth
with what I think now was not just anger but a kind

of terror on his face, an animal wildness
in the eyes and the jaw tight, making ropes in his neck
while in a long blur with his left hand raised and gripping
an iron file he is moving toward the men who wait
attentive and motionless as deer trembling in a clearing,
and instantly there is my father between Bobby
and the men as if he were waking them after a long sleep,
reaching out to touch the shoulder of the blond one
as he says in a voice almost terrible in its gentleness,
its discretion, *you boys will have to leave now.*
He takes one look at Bobby who is shrinking back
into the shadows of the Hobbs, then walks quickly back
to his office at the front of the shop, and soon
the black Corvette with the orange California plates
is squealing onto Highway 54 heading west into the sun.

IV.

So there they are, as I will always remember them,
the men who were once fullbacks or tackles or guards
in their three-point stances knuckling into the mud,
hungry for high school glory and the pride of their fathers,
eager *to gallop terribly against each other's bodies,*
each man in his body looking out now at the nakedness
of a body like his, men who each autumn had followed

their fathers into the pheasant-rich fields of Kansas
and as boys had climbed down from the Allis-Chalmers
after plowing their first straight furrow, licking the dirt
from their lips, the hand of the father resting lightly
upon their shoulder, men who in the oven-warm winter
kitchens of Baptist households saw after a bath the body
of the father and felt diminished by it, who that same
winter in the abandoned schoolyard felt the odd intimacy
of their fist against the larger boy's cheekbone
but kept hitting, ferociously, and walked away
feeling for the first time the strength, the *abundance,*
of their own bodies. And I imagine the men
that evening after the strangest day of their lives,
after they have left the shop without speaking
and made the long drive home alone in their pickups,
I see them in their little white frame houses on the edge
of town adrift in the long silence of the evening turning
finally to their wives, touching without speaking the hair
which she has learned to let fall about her shoulders
at this hour of night, lifting the white nightgown
from her body as she in turn unbuttons his work shirt
heavy with the sweat and grease of the day's labor until
they stand naked before each other and begin to touch
in a slow choreography of familiar gestures their bodies,
she touching his chest, his hand brushing her breasts,
and he does not say the word *beautiful* because

he cannot and never has, and she does not say it
because it would embarrass him or any other man
she has ever known, though it is precisely the word
I am thinking now as I stand before Donatello's *David*
with my wife touching my sleeve, *what are you thinking?*
and I think of the letter from my father years ago
describing the death of Bobby Sudduth, a single shot
from a twelve-gauge which he held against his chest,
the death of the heart, I suppose, *a kind of terrible beauty,*
as someone said of the death of Hart Crane, though that is
surely a perverse use of the word, and I was stunned then,
thinking of the damage men will visit upon their bodies,
what are you thinking? she asks again, and so I begin
to tell her about a strange afternoon in Kansas,
about something I have never spoken of, and we walk
to a window where the shifting light spreads a sheen
along the casement, and looking out, we see the city
blazing like miles of uncut wheat, the farthest buildings
taken in their turn, and the great dome, the way
the metal roof of the machine shop, I tell her,
would break into flame late on an autumn day, with such beauty.

The Invisible Man

We are kids with orange Jujubes stuck to our chins
and licorice sticks snaking out of our jeans pockets,
and we see him, or rather don't see him, when the bandages
uncoil from his face and lo, there's nothing between
the hat and suit. It is wonderful, this pure nothing,
but we begin to be troubled by the paradoxes of nonexistence.
(Can he pee? If he itches, can he scratch? If he eats
Milk Duds, do they disappear?) Sure, standing around
in the girls' locker room unobserved or floating erasers
in math class, who could resist, but the enigma
of sheer absence, the loss of the body, of *who we are,*
continues to grind against us even into the Roy Rogers
western that follows. The pungent VistaVision embodiments
of good and evil—this clear-eyed young man with watermelon
voice and high principles, the fat, unshaven dipshits
with no respect for old ladies or hard-working Baptist
farmers—none of this feels quite solid anymore. Granted,
it's the world as the world appears, but *provisional* somehow,
a shadow, a ghost, dragging behind every rustled cow
or runaway stagecoach, and though afterward the cloud
of insubstantiality lifts and fades as we stroll out
grimacing into the hard sunlight, there is that
slight tremble of déjàvu years later in Philosophy 412
as Professor Caws mumbles on about essence and existence,
being and nothingness, and *Happy Trails to You* echoes
from the far end of the hall.

In *The Invisible Man*
sometimes we could see the thread or thin wire that lifted
the gun from the thief's hand, and at the Hearst mansion
only days ago a sign explained that the orchestra
of Leonard Slye entertained the zillionaire and his Hollywood
friends on spring evenings caressed by ocean breezes
and the scent of gardenias. You can almost see them swaying
to "Mood Indigo" or "Cherokee," champagne glasses in hand:
Chaplin, Gable, Marion Davies, Herman Mankiewicz,
and cruising large as the *Titanic,* William Randolph Hearst,
Citizen Kane himself. Leonard Slye sees this too, along with
the Roman statuary and rare medieval tapestries, and thinks,
someday, someday, and becomes invisible so that he
can appear later as Roy Rogers and make movies in
Victorville, California, where Mankiewicz and Orson Welles
will write the story of an enormous man who misplaced
his childhood and tried to call it back on his deathbed.
O Leonard Slye, lifting Roy's six-gun from its holster,
O Hearst, dreaming of Rosebud and raping the castles of Europe,
O America, with your dreams of money and power,
small boys sit before your movie screens invisible
to themselves, waiting for the next episode, in which they
stumble blind into daylight and the body of the world.

All the People in Hopper's Paintings

All the people in Hopper's paintings walk by me
here in the twilight the way our neighbors
would stroll by of an evening in my hometown
smiling and waving as I leaned against
the front-porch railing and hated them all
and the place I had grown up in. I smoked
my Pall Mall with a beautifully controlled rage
in the manner of James Dean and imagined
life beyond the plains in the towns of Hopper
where people were touched by the light of the real.

The people in Hopper's paintings were lonely
as I was and lived in brown rooms whose
long, sad windows looked out on the roofs
of brown buildings in the towns that made
them lonely. Or they lived in coffee shops
and cafés at 3 a.m under decadent flowers
of cigarette smoke as I thought I would have
if there had been such late-night conspiracy
in the town that held me but offered nothing.
And now they gather around with their bland,

mysterious faces in half-shadow, many still
bearing the hard plane of light that found them
from the left side of the room, as in Vermeer,

others wearing the dark splotches of early
evening across their foreheads and chins that said
they were, like me, tragic, dark, undiscovered:
the manicurist from the barber shop buried
beneath a pyramid of light and a clock frozen
at eleven, the woman sitting on the bed
too exhausted with the hopelessness of brick walls

and barber poles and Rhinegold ads to dress
herself in street clothes. The wordless, stale
affair with the filling station attendant
was the anteroom to heartbreak. The gloom
of his stupid uniform and black tie beneath
the three white bulbs blinking MOBILGAS into
the woods that loomed bleak as tombstones
on the edge of town; the drab backroom
with its Prestone cans and sighing Vargas girls
and grease rags; his panting, pathetic *loneliness*.

But along the white island of the station,
the luminous squares from its windows
lying quietly like carpets on the pavement
had been my hope, my sense then of the real world
beyond the familiar one, like the blazing cafe
of the nighthawks casting the town into shadow,

or the beach house of the sea watchers
who sat suspended on a verandah of light,
stunned by the flat, hard sea of the real.
Everywhere was that phosphorescence, that pale

wash of promise lifting roofs and chimneys
out of dullness, out of the ordinary that I
could smell in my work clothes coming home
from a machine shop lined with men who stood
at lathes and looked out of windows and wore
the same late-afternoon layers of sunlight
that Hopper's people carried to hotel rooms
and cafeterias. Why was their monotony
blessed, their melancholy apocalyptic, while
my days hung like red rags from my pockets

as I stood, welding torch in hand, and searched
the horizon with the eyes and straight mouth
of Hopper's women? If they had come walking
toward me, those angels of boredom, if they
had arrived clothed in their robes of light,
would I have recognized them? If all those women
staring out of windows had risen from their desks
and unmade beds, and the men from their offices
and sun-draped brownstones, would I have known?
Would I have felt their light hands touching

my face the way infants do when people
seem no more real than dreams or picture books?
The girl in the blue gown leaning from her door
at high noon, the gray-haired gentleman
in the hotel by the railroad, holding his cigarette
so delicately, they have found me, and we
walk slowly through the small Kansas town
that held me and offered nothing, where the light
fell through the windows of brown rooms, and people
looked out, strangely, as if they had been painted there.

The Book of Hours

Like the blue angels of the nativity, the museum patrons
hover around the art historian, who has arrived frazzled
and limp after waking late in her boyfriend's apartment.
And here, she notes, *the Procession of St. Gregory,*
where atop Hadrian's mausoleum the angel of death
returns his bloody sword to its scabbard, and staring
down at the marble floor, liquid in the slanted
silver light of midmorning, she ponders briefly
the polished faces of her audience: seraphim gazing
heavenward at the golden throne, or, as she raises
her tired eyes to meet their eyes, the evolving souls
of purgatory, bored as the inhabitants of some
fashionable European spa sunbathing on boulders.
And here, notice the lovely treatment of St. John
on Patmos, robed in blue and gold, and she tells the story
of gallnuts, goats' skins dried and stretched into vellum—
the word *vellum* delicious in its saying, caressed
in her mouth like a fat breakfast plum—lapis lazuli
crushed into pools of ultramarine blue, and gold foil
hammered thin enough to float upon the least breath,
the scribes hastily scraping gold flakes into ceramic cups,
curling their toes against the cold like her lover stepping
out of bed in that odd, delicate way of his, wisps of gold
drifting like miniature angels onto the scriptorium's
stone floor, and dog's teeth to polish the gold leaf

as transcendent in its beauty, she says, *as the medieval*
mind conceived the soul to be.

                      The patrons are beginning
to wander now as she points to the crucifixion scene,
done to perfection by the Limbourg brothers, the skull and bones
of Adam lying scattered beneath the Roman soldier's horse,
and the old custodian wipes palm prints from the glass, the monks
breathe upon their fingertips and pray against the hard winter,
and the art historian recalls the narrow shafts of light tapping
the breakfast table, the long curve of his back in half-shadow,
the bed's rumpled sheets lifted by an ocean breeze
as if they were the weightless gold leaf of the spirit.

Cigarettes

Gross, loathsome. Trays and plates loaded
like rain gutters, butts crumpled and damp with gin,
ashes still shedding the rank breath of exhaustion—
nevertheless, an integral part of human evolution,
like reading. Cigarettes possess the nostalgic potency
of old songs: hand on the steering wheel, fat pack
of Pall Malls snug under my sleeve, skinny bicep
pressed against the car door so my muscle bulges,
and my girl, wanting a smoke, touches my arm.
Or 3 a.m. struggling with the Chekhov paper, I break
the blue stamp with my thumb, nudge open petals of foil,
and the bloom of nicotine puts me right back in the feedstore
where my grandfather used to trade—leather, oats, burlap,
and red sawdust. Or at the beach, minute flares floating
in the deep dark, rising, falling in the hands of aunts
and uncles telling the old stories, drowsy with beer,
waves lapping the sand and dragging their voices down.
Consider the poverty of lungs drawing ordinary air,
the unreality of it, the lie it tells about quotidian existence.
Bad news craves cigarettes, whole heaps of them, sucking
in the bad air the way the drowning gulp river water,
though in hospital rooms I've seen grief let smoke
gather slowly into pools that rise, and rise again
to nothing. I've studied the insincere purity
of a mouth without the cigarette that gives the air form,
the hand focus, the lips a sense of identity.
The way Shirley Levin chattered after concerts:

her fingers mimicking piano keys and the cigarette
they held galloping in heart-like fibrillations until
the thrill of it had unravelled in frayed strands of smoke.
1979: "Sweet Lorraine," seventh, eighth chorus, and
I'm looking at the small black scallops above the keyboard,
a little history of smoke and jazz, improvisation as
a kind of forgetting. The music of cigarettes:
dawn stirs and lifts the smoke in dove-gray striations
that hang, then break, scatter, and regroup along
the sill where paperbacks warp in sunlight and the cat
claws house spiders. Cigarettes are the only way
to make bleakness nutritional, or at least useful,
something to do while feeling terrified. They cling
to the despair of certain domestic scenes—my father,
for instance, smoking L&M's all night in the kitchen,
a sea of smoke risen to neck level as I wander in
like some small craft drifting and lost in fog
while a distant lighthouse flares awhile and swings away.
Yes, they kill you, but so do television and bureaucrats
and the drugged tedium of certain rooms piped
with tasteful music where we have all sat waiting
for someone to enter with a silver plate laden
with Camels and Lucky Strikes, someone who leans
into our ears and tells us that the day's work is done,
and done well, offers us black coffee in white cups,
and whispers the way trees whisper, *yes, yes, oh yes.*

The Himalayas

The stewardess' dream of the Himalayas
followed her everywhere: from Omaha
to Baltimore and back, and then to Seattle
and up and down the California coast until
she imagined herself strapped to the wing
just across from seat 7A muttering
little homemade mantras and shivering
in the cold, stiff wind of the inexpressible.
It could hardly go on like this, she thought,
the unending prayer to nothing in particular
whirling around in her head while she held
the yellow mask over her face and demonstrated
correct breathing techniques: the point was
to breathe calmly like angels observing
the final separation of light from a dead star,
or the monk described in the travel book
trying to untangle his legs and stand once more
at the mouth of his cave. The stewardess
delighted in her symmetrical gestures, the dance
of her hands describing the emergency exits
and the overhead lights that made exquisite
small cones in the night for readers and children
afraid of the dark. As the passengers fell asleep
around her, the stewardess reached up to adjust
the overhead whose cone of light rose over her

like some miniature white peak of the Himalayas
as if she were a cave in the Himalayas,
the cave of her own body, perhaps, in which
she sat patiently now, looking out, waiting.

Body and Soul

Half-numb, guzzling bourbon and Coke from coffee mugs,
our fathers fall in love with their own stories, nuzzling
the facts but mauling the truth, and my friend's father begins
to lay out with the slow ease of a blues ballad a story
about sandlot baseball in Commerce, Oklahoma, decades ago.
These were men's teams, grown men, some in their thirties
and forties who worked together in zinc mines or on oil rigs,
sweat and khaki and long beers after work, steel guitar music
whanging in their ears, little white rent houses to return to
where their wives complained about money and broken Kenmores
and then said the hell with it and sang "Body and Soul"
in the bathtub and later that evening with the kids asleep
lay in bed stroking their husband's wrist tattoo and smoking
Chesterfields from a fresh pack until everything was OK.
Well, you get the idea. Life goes on, the next day is Sunday,
another ball game, and the other team shows up one man short.

They say, we're one man short, but can we use this boy,
he's only fifteen years old, and at least he'll make a game.
They take a look at the kid, muscular and kind of knowing
the way he holds his glove, with the shoulders loose,
the thick neck, but then with that boy's face under
a clump of angelic blond hair, and say, oh, hell, sure,
let's play ball. So it all begins, the men loosening up,
joking about the fat catcher's sex life, it's so bad
last night he had to sleep with his wife, that sort of thing,

pairing off into little games of catch that heat up into
throwing matches, the smack of the fungo bat, lazy jogging
into right field, big smiles and arcs of tobacco juice,
and the talk that gives cool, easy feeling to the air,
talk among men normally silent, normally brittle and a little
angry with the empty promise of their lives. But they chatter
and say rock and fire, babe, easy out, and go right ahead
and pitch to the boy, but nothing fancy, just hard fastballs
right around the belt, and the kid takes the first two
but on the third pops the bat around so quick and sure
that they pause a moment before turning around to watch
the ball still rising and finally dropping far beyond
the abandoned tractor that marks left field. Holy shit.
They're pretty quiet watching him round the bases,
but then, what the hell, the kid knows how to hit a ball,
so what, let's play some goddamned baseball here.
And so it goes. The next time up, the boy gets a look
at a very nifty low curve, then a slider, and the next one
is the curve again, and he sends it over the Allis-Chalmers,
high and big and sweet. The left fielder just stands there, frozen.
As if this isn't enough, the next time up he bats left-handed.
They can't believe it, and the pitcher, a tall, mean-faced
man from Okarche who just doesn't give a shit anyway
because his wife ran off two years ago leaving him with
three little ones and a rusted-out Dodge with a cracked block,
leans in hard, looking at the fat catcher like he was the sonofabitch

who ran off with his wife, leans in and throws something
out of the dark, green hell of forbidden fastballs, something
that comes in at the knees and then leaps viciously toward
the kid's elbow. He swings exactly the way he did right-handed,
and they all turn like a chorus line toward deep right field
where the ball loses itself in sagebrush and the sad burnt,
dust of dustbowl Oklahoma. It is something to see.

But why make a long story long: runs pile up on both sides,
the boy comes around five times, and five times the pitcher
is cursing both God and His mother as his chew of tobacco sours
into something resembling horse piss, and a ragged and bruised
Spalding baseball disappears into the far horizon. Goodnight,
Irene. They have lost the game and some painful side bets
and they have been suckered. And it means nothing to them
though it should to you when they are told the boy's name is
Mickey Mantle. And that's the story, and those are the facts.
But the facts are not the truth. I think, though, as I scan
the faces of these old men now lost in the innings of their youth,
I think I know what the truth of this story is, and I imagine
it lying there in the weeds behind that Allis-Chalmers
just waiting for the obvious question to be asked: why, oh
why in hell didn't they just throw around the kid, walk him,
after he hit the third homer? Anybody would have,
especially nine men with disappointed wives and dirty socks
and diminishing expectations for whom winning at anything

meant everything. Men who knew how to play the game,
who had talent when the other team had nothing except this ringer
who without a pitch to hit was meaningless, and they could go home
with their little two-dollar side bets and stride into the house
with a bottle of Southern Comfort under their arms and grab
Dixie or May Ella up and dance across the gray linoleum
as if it were V-Day all over again. But they did not.
And they did not because they were men, and this was a boy.
And they did not because sometimes after making love,
after smoking their Chesterfields in the cool silence and
listening to the big bands on the radio that sounded so glamorous,
so distant, they glanced over at their wives and noticed the lines
growing heavier around the eyes and mouth, felt what their wives
felt: that Les Brown and Glenn Miller and all those dancing couples
and in fact all possibility of human gaiety and light-heartedness
were as far away and unreachable as Times Square or the Avalon
Ballroom. They did not because of the gray linoleum lying there
in the half-dark, the free calendar from the local mortuary
that said one day was pretty much like another, the work gloves
looped over the doorknob like dead squirrels. And they did not
because they had gone through a depression and a war that had left
them with the idea that being a man in the eyes of their fathers
and everyone else had cost them just too goddamned much to lay it
at the feet of a fifteen-year-old boy. And so they did not walk him,
and lost, but at least had some ragged remnant of themselves
to take back home. But there is one thing more, though it is not

a fact. When I see my friend's father staring hard into the bottomless
well of home plate as Mantle's fifth homer heads toward Arkansas,
I know that this man with the half-orphaned children and
worthless Dodge has also encountered for his first and possibly
only time the vast gap between talent and genius, has seen
as few have in the harsh light of an Oklahoma Sunday, the blond
and blue-eyed bringer of truth, who will not easily be forgiven.

Airlifting Horses

Boy soldiers gawk and babble, eyes rapt
in what seems like worship as the horses rise
in the bludgeoned air. A brushfire is swarming
roads and highways, and the last way out is up

or a flatboat in the lagoon. We used to drop
the reins and let them race there, hurdling
driftwood, heaps of kelp, waves lapping the sand
in a lace maker's weave of sea and foam.

Now they're startled into flight, and the air,
stunned and savaged by the propeller's flail,
beats us back. Its sudden thunder must be a storm
their skins have for the first time failed to sense.

Cowering beneath the blades, we have cradled them
like babies, strapped them in slings strong enough
to lug trucks, and their silence is the purest tone
of panic. Their great necks crane and arch,

the eyes flame, and their spidery shadows,
big-bellied and stiff-legged, swallow us,
then dwindle to blotches on the tarmac
as they lift. The cable that hauls them up

like some kind of spiritual harness vanishes
from sight. Their hooves pummel the heavy wind,
and the earth they rode a thousand days or more
falls away in hunks of brown and yellow.

Even the weight of their bodies has abandoned them,
but now they are the gods we always wanted:
winged as any myth, strange, distant, real,
and we will never be ourselves till they return.

Old Men Playing Basketball

The heavy bodies lunge, the broken language
of fake and drive, glamorous jump shot
slowed to a stutter. Their gestures, in love
again with the pure geometry of curves,

rise towards the ball, falter, and fall away.
On the boards their hands and fingertips
tremble in tense little prayers of reach
and balance. Then, the grind of bone

and socket, the caught breath, the sigh,
the grunt of the body laboring to give
birth to itself. In their toiling and grand
sweeps, I wonder, do they still make love

to their wives, kissing the undersides
of their wrists, dancing the old soft-shoe
of desire? And on the long walk home
from the VFW, do they still sing

to the drunken moon? Stands full, clock
moving, the one in Army fatigues
and houseshoes says to himself, *pick and roll,*
and the phrase sounds musical as ever,

radio crooning songs of love after the game,
the girl leaning back in the Chevy's front seat
as her raven hair flames in the shuddering
light of the outdoor movie, and now he drives,

gliding toward the net. A glass wand
of autumn light breaks over the backboard.
Boys rise up in old men, wings begin to sprout
at their backs. The ball turns in the darkening air.

Old Women

They of the trembling hands and liver spots
like a map of Asia, far pale countries of the flesh
wandering as their hands wandered beside me
over texts of Ezekiel and Jeremiah to prophesy
the blues and yellows of next summer's swallowtails
any Sunday morning in the First Methodist Church
of Liberal, Kansas, where I, boy lepidopterist,
future nomad of the lost countries of imagination,
felt the hand on my wrist, the Black Sea of not forgetting.

Mrs. Tate, for instance, stunning the dusty air
with "Casta Diva" in the tar-paper shack's backyard
littered with lenses, trays, tripods, the rusted remains
of camera equipment strewn with drunken care
by her husband, artist and disciple of Lewis Hine,
now failed in his craft but applauding his wife's
shrill arias Friday nights when the deaf town died
to rise again on Sunday and a boy listened across
the road to what might be, he thought, happiness.

The nameless one, garbage picker, hag of the alleys,
the town's bad dream scavenging trash cans
at 3 a.m. while I, sneaking from bed, edged closer
in the shadows, and she in her legendary madness
clawed through egg cartons, bottles, headless dolls.
Junk madonna in a high school formal, she cried

her lover's name, turning then with outspread hands,
reaching to hold my head against her hard breast,
sour smell of old crinoline, the terror of love.

And Miss Harp, bent over a cup of steaming tea,
sipping a novel fat as Falstaff, wheezing, thick-lensed,
sister of the holy order of spinster librarians,
cousin to the brothers Karamazov and Becky Sharp.
She called out my name, her piccolo voice doing
scales, and handed me an armload of new arrivals:
Doctor Zhivago, Kon-Tiki, A Boy's Guide to Aeronautics.
Her watery eyes bloomed, her quavering hand nudged
my shoulder: *Russia, adventure, the mystery of flight.*

Mazurkas drift down from the gazebo, troikas
clatter along the dark avenues of Yalta lined with
cypresses and firs. Behind a hedge of blackthorn
we stroll the esplanade as a sexton tolls the bell
of some distant church. Mrs. Tate unfurls her
unnecessary parasol, and the librarian remarks
the harsh ocean air that fogs the street lamps.
A third woman takes my arm, humming lightly,
smiling, her porcelain hand calm upon my wrist.

Song

Gesang ist Dasein.

A small thing done well, the steel bit paring
the cut end of the collar, lifting delicate
blue spirals of iron slowly out of lamplight

into darkness until they broke and fell
into a pool of oil and water below.
A small thing done well, my father said

so often that I tired of hearing it and lost
myself in the shop's north end, an underworld
of welders who wore black masks and stared

through smoked glass where all was midnight
except the purest spark, the blue-white arc
of the clamp and rod. Hammers made dull tunes

hacking slag, and acetylene flames cast shadows
of men against the tin roof like great birds
trapped in diminishing circles of light.

Each day was like another. I stood beside him
and watched the lathe spin on, coils of iron
climbing into dusk, the file's drone, the rasp,

and finally the honing cloth with its small song
of things done well that I would carry into sleep
and dreams of men with wings of fire and steel.

Bert Fairchild, 1906–1990

Thermoregulation in Winter Moths

How do the winter moths survive when other moths die?
What enables them to avoid freezing as they rest,
and what makes it possible for them to fly—and so
to seek food and mates—in the cold?

—BERNDT HEINRICH, *SCIENTIFIC AMERICAN*

1. The Himalayas

The room lies there, immaculate, bone light
on white walls, shell-pink carpet, and pale, too,
are the wrists and hands of professors gathered
in the outer hall where behind darkness
and a mirror they can observe unseen.
They were told: high in the Himalayas
Buddhist monks thrive in subzero cold
far too harsh for human life. Suspended
in the deep grace of meditation, they raise
their body heat and do not freeze to death.
So five Tibetan monks have been flown
to Cambridge and the basement of Reed Hall.
They sit now with crossed legs and slight smiles,
and white sheets lap over their shoulders
like enfolded wings. The sheets are wet,
and drops of water trickle down the monks'
bare backs. The professors wait patiently
but with the widened eyes of fathers
watching new babies in hospital cribs.
Their aluminum clipboards rest gently

in their laps, their pens are poised,
and in a well-lit room in Cambridge
five Tibetan monks sit under heavy wet sheets
and steam begins to rise from their shoulders.

2. Burn Ward

My friend speaks haltingly, the syllables freezing
against the night air because the nurse's story
still possesses him, the ease with which she tended
patients so lost in pain, so mangled, scarred, and
abandoned in some arctic zone of uncharted suffering
that strangers stumbling onto the ward might
cry out, rushing back to a world where the very air
did not grieve flesh. *Empathy was impossible,*
he said. A kind of fog or frozen lake lay between her
and the patient, far away. Empathy was an insult,
to look into the eyes of the consumed and pretend,
I know. It must have been this lake, this vast
glacial plain that she would never cross, where
the patient waved in the blue-gray distance,
alone and trembling the way winter moths tremble
to warm themselves, while she stood, also alone
and freezing, on the other side, it must have been

this unbearable cold that made her drive straight home
one day, sit down cross-legged in the center of
an empty garage, pour the gasoline on like a balm,
and calmly strike a match like someone starting
a winter fire, or lost and searching in the frozen dark.

Keats

I knew him. He ran the lathe next to mine.
Perfectionist, a madman, even on overtime
Saturday night. Hum of the crowd floating
from the ballpark, shouts, slamming doors
from the bar down the street, he would lean
into the lathe and make a little song
with the honing cloth, rubbing the edges,
smiling like a man asleep, dreaming.
A short guy, but fearless. At Margie's
he would take no lip, put the mechanic big
as a Buick through a stack of crates out back
and walked away with a broken thumb
but never said a word. Marge was a loud,
dirty girl with booze breath and bad manners.
He loved her. One night late I saw them in
the kitchen dancing something like a rhumba
to the radio, dishtowels wrapped around
their heads like swamis. Their laughter chimed
rich as brass rivets rolling down a tin roof.
But it was the work that kept him out of fights,
and I remember the red hair flaming
beneath the lamp, calipers measuring out
the last cut, his hands flicking iron burrs
like shooting stars through the shadows.
It was the iron, cut to a perfect fit, smooth
as bone china and gleaming under lamplight

that made him stand back, take out a smoke,
and sing. It was the dust that got him, his lungs
collapsed from breathing in a life of work.
Lying there, his hands are what I can't forget.

The Ascension of Ira Campbell

So there was Campbell rising in a scream
on the yellow traveling block that carried
five thousand feet of drill pipe in and out
of the hard summer earth that abideth ever,
paperback *Tractatus* sticking from his hip pocket.
Student and roughneck, Campbell dug his gloves
into the gray swag of metaphysics
and came up empty, but here on the wordless
and wind-flattened high plains he sang,
Whereof one cannot speak, thereof one must
be silent. He toiled, looting every
proposition for its true spirit, said
it was the end of language, the dark rustle
of the soul's wings that would haul the mind
beyond meaning. *It's all here, Fairchild,*
he screamed, waving the red book above his head,
the cables moaning, Campbell ascending
into the cloud-strewn facts of the sky,
blue or not blue, a sky amazingly itself.

The Dumka

His parents would sit alone together
on the blue divan in the small living room
listening to Dvořák's piano quintet.
They would sit there in their old age,
side by side, quite still, backs rigid, hands
in their laps, and look straight ahead
at the yellow light of the phonograph
that seemed as distant as a lamplit
window seen across the plains late at night.
They would sit quietly as something dense

and radiant swirled around them, something
like the dust storms of the thirties that began
by smearing the sky green with doom
but afterward drenched the air with an amber
glow and then vanished, leaving profiles
of children on pillows and a pale gauze
over mantles and tabletops. But it was
the memory of dust that encircled them now
and made them smile faintly and raise
or bow their heads as they spoke about

the farm in twilight with piano music
spiraling out across red roads and fields
of maize, bread lines in the city, women
and men lining main street like mannequins,

and then the war, the white frame rent house,
and the homecoming, the homecoming,
the homecoming, and afterward, green lawns
and a new piano with its mahogany gleam
like pond ice at dawn, and now alone
in the house in the vanishing neighborhood,

the slow mornings of coffee and newspapers
and evenings of music and scattered bits
of talk like leaves suddenly fallen before
one notices the new season. And they would sit
there alone and soon he would reach across
and lift her hand as if it were the last unbroken
leaf and he would hold her hand in his hand
for a long time and they would look far off
into the music of their lives as they sat alone
together in the room in the house in Kansas.

A Model of Downtown Los Angles, 1940

It's a bright, guilty world.

—ORSON WELLES IN *THE LADY FROM SHANGHAI*

But there is no water.

—T. S. ELIOT, *THE WASTE LAND*

The oldest Mercedes in California adorns
the crowded foyer of the L.A. County Museum
of Natural History, and babies shriek like bats
in the elevator that lowers my daughter
and me to the basement. There, among the faint,
intermingled drifts of ammonia and urine
from the men's room, phantom display lights
luring shadows over the inventions of Edison
and Bell, and dusty monuments to a century
of industrial progress, lies the mock-up L.A.,

whose perusal has been assigned to my daughter's
fourth-grade class in California history.
Fallen into ruin, its plexiglass sky yellowing
and covered with cracks, the fault lines of heaven,
it is soon to be hauled off with the duplicate
rhino horns and kachina dolls dulled with varnish.
Sarah circles the city, her face looming
large as a god's over buildings, across avenues
and boulevards from Vignes to Macy, then back
around to the borders of Beaudry and Eighth Street,

where in 1938 my father sat alone
in the Tiptop Diner and made tomato soup
from a free bowl of hot water and catsup.
Across the street was the office of the L.A. *Times*
where several upstanding Christian men had conspired
to steal the water from the Owens Valley.
Our farm became a scrap yard of rotted pears,
a bone yard, irrigation canals dried up
and turned to sage. A thousand lives in ruin
while L.A.'s San Fernando Valley rose

from desert into orange groves and, overnight,
made a fortune for the city fathers. One day
our hayrack caught fire and there was hell
in the air. On the roof, my father saw
in the distance a Hindu city with camels,
water buffalo, and four elephants: *Gunga Din*.
Water gone, vultures circling, Hollywood
was moving in. We followed Mulholland's
aqueduct south to L.A. and the cool dark
of the Pantages Theatre in blazing August

while my father hunted for cheap housing,
shacks with swamp boxes near Echo Park.
Each day he rode the classifieds until
the bars looked better, drank warm Pabst

at Mickey's Hideout where Franz Werfel
sang Verdi arias and told him stories
of Garbo, Brecht, Huxley, and Thomas Mann.
Later, he worked the rigs on Signal Hill
for a dollar a day, slinging the pipe tongs
and coming home smelling of oil and mud.

The days: morning light opening the streets
like a huge hand, then the bruised fist
of evening, that incredible pink and blue
bleeding into night, and the homeless
in Pershing Square claiming their benches again.
That summer he was shipped to Okinawa,
the Japanese trucked like crates of oranges
to Manzanar near Lone Pine in the Owens Valley,
and I wandered among the jacarandas
and birds-of-paradise at the Public Library

reading *The Communist Manifesto*
and plotting revenge. But I was a child.
Now I study Blake's *Songs* in rare editions
at Huntington's Library and Botanical Gardens
and imagine the great patron and his pals
looking down on L.A. from the verandah
and sighing, *Bill Mulholland made this city,*
as the sun pales once more beneath a purple fist.

So, here is the Hall of Records, and Union Station
where my father, returned from the Pacific,

swore that we would head back north again.
Last night on television a man named Rodney King
showed how the city had progressed beyond
its primitive beginnings, how the open hand
of the law could touch a man in his very bones.
And there, staring back from the west end
of Spring Street, is my daughter learning her lessons
as she bends down for a closer look, pale blue eyes
descending slowly over the city, setting like
twin suns above the Department of Water and Power.

The Children

. . . genially, Magoo-like, when in the street he might pat the
heads of water hydrants and parking meters, taking these to
be the heads of children.

—OLIVER SACKS,

THE MAN WHO MISTOOK HIS WIFE FOR A HAT

More than children: frail, disheveled angels,
the awful weight of their wings shrugged off,
light feet again in love with the earth. They sing
some celestial liturgy too brittle for my ears
and guard the souls of commuters from the beasts
that would otherwise surely drive them into hell.
As they stand against the Plymouths of this world,
the clock of eternity is upon their foreheads
and a red arrow will point them homeward again.
But for now, humming their requiem to human memory,
they usher me toward the vanishing point.
That there should be such beautiful little ones!
symmetrically arranged like the found objects
in Cornell's boxes—a postcard from Paris,
a thimble, the King of Diamonds, a porcelain doll.
I follow them along the streets whose names
are only trees to me, past the toy shop remembered
and forgotten repeatedly. As in a dream,
my own home, vaguely familiar, drifts toward me
buoyed by the music of my past: the *Kinderscenen*,
or mazurkas to annoy my father and wake up the cats.
As the poet of children wrote, *the altering eye*

alters all, for I was a boy of vision,
and childhood was a scene from *The Magic Flute.*

Here is my wife, the green Homburg floating
across the verandah, to guide me up the steps
that seem suddenly like the backs of turtles
returning to the open sea. Here are my paintings
giving onto pools and glades that only I can know,
and my old Bösendorfer with its ancient brown tones.
The chords rise beneath my fingers, a seamless
harmony between the seer and the seen, the spirit's
body, the body's prayer.
                              Evening drops down.
I sing the *Dichterliebe,* and my wife accompanies.
Outside, the voices of children are heard in the rain,
Und Nebelbilder steigen / Wohl aus der Erd hervor,
and misty images rise / from the earth.

Little Boy

The sun lowers on our backyard in Kansas,
and I am looking up through the circling spokes
of a bicycle asking my father as mindlessly
as I would ask if he ever saw DiMaggio or Mantle
why we dropped the bomb on those two towns
in Japan, and his face goes all wooden, the eyes
freezing like rabbits in headlights, the palm
of his hand slowly tapping the arm of a lawn chair
that has appeared in family photographs
since 1945, the shadow of my mother thrown
across it, the green Packard in the background
which my father said he bought because after Saipan
and Tinian and Okinawa, "I felt like they owed it to me."
These were names I didn't know, islands distant
as planets, anonymous. Where is Saipan?
Where is Okinawa? Where is the Pacific?
Could you see the cloud in the air like the smoke
from Eugene Messenbaum's semi, that huge cloud
when he rolled it out on Highway 54 last winter?
The hand is hammering the chair arm, beating it,
and I know it's all wrong as I move backward
on the garage floor and watch his eyes watching
the sun in its evening burial and the spreading
silver light and then darkness over the farms
and vast, flat fields which I will grow so tired of,
so weary of years later that I will leave, watching

then as I do now his eyes as they take in the falling rag
of the sun, a level stare, a gaze that asks nothing
and gives nothing, the sun burning itself to ashes
constantly, the orange maize blackening in drought
and waste, and he can do nothing and neither can I.

The Welder, Visited by the Angel of Mercy

Something strange is the soul on the earth.

—GEORG TRAKL

Spilled melons rotting on the highway's shoulder sweeten
the air, their bruised rinds silvering under the half-moon.
A blown tire makes the pickup list into the shoulder
like a swamped boat, and the trailer that was torn loose

has a twisted tongue and hitch that he has cut away,
trimmed, and wants to weld back on. Beyond lie fields
of short grass where cattle moan and drift like clouds, hunks
of dark looming behind barbed wire. The welder, crooning

along with a Patsy Cline tune from the truck's radio,
smokes his third joint, and a cracked bottle of Haig & Haig
glitters among the weeds, the rank and swollen melons.
Back at St. Benedict's they're studying Augustine now,

the great rake in his moment sobbing beneath the fig trees,
the child somewhere singing, take and read, take and read.
What they are not doing is fucking around in a ditch
on the road to El Paso ass-deep in mushmelons

and a lame pickup packed with books that are scattered now
from hell to breakfast. Jesus. Flipping the black mask up,
he reaches into the can for a fresh rod, clamps it,
then stares into the evening sky. Stars. The blackened moon.

The red dust of the city at night. Roy Garcia,
a man in a landscape, tries to weld his truck and his life
back together, but forgetting to drop the mask back down,
he touches rod to iron, and the arc's flash hammers

his eyes as he stumbles, blind, among the fruit of the earth.
The flame raging through his brain spreads its scorched wings
in a dazzle of embers, lowering the welder, the good student,
into his grass bed, where the world lies down to sleep

until it wakes once more into the dream of Being:
Roy and Maria at breakfast, white cups of black coffee,
fresh melons in blue bowls, the books in leather bindings
standing like silent children along the western wall.

The Death of a Small Town

It's rather like snow: in the beginning,
immaculate, brilliant, the trees shocked
into a crystalline awareness of something

remarkable, like them, but not of them,
perfectly formed and yet formless.
You want to walk up and down in it,

this bleak, maizeless field of innocence
with its black twigs and blue leaves.
You want to feel the silence crunching

beneath your houseshoes, but soon everyone
is wallowing in it, the trees no longer
bear sunlight, the sky has dragged down

its gray dream, and now it's no longer snow
but something else, not water or even
its dumb cousin, mud, but something used,

ordinary, dull. Then one morning at 4 a.m.
you go out seeking that one feeble remnant,
you are so lonely, and of course you find

its absence. An odd thing, to come upon
an absence, to come upon a death, to come upon
what is left when everything is gone.

The Art of the Lathe

Leonardo invented the first one.
The next was a pole lathe with a drive cord,
illustrated in Plumier's *L'art de tourner en perfection*.
Then Ramsden, Vauconson, the great Maudslay,
his student Roberts, Fox, Clement, Whitworth.

The long line of machinists to my left
lean into their work, ungloved hands adjusting the calipers,
tapping the bit lightly with their fingertips.
Each man withdraws into his house of work:
the rough cut, shearing of iron by tempered steel,
blue-black threads lifting like locks of hair,
then breaking over bevel and ridge.
Oil and water splash over the whitening bit, hissing.
The lathe on night shift, moonlight silvering the bed-ways.

The journeyman I apprenticed with, Roy Garcia,
in silk shirt, khakis, and Florsheims. Cautious,
almost delicate explanations and slow,
shapely hand movements. Craft by repetition.
Haig & Haig behind the tool chest.

In Diderot's *Encyclopédie*, an engraving
of a small machine shop: forge and bellows in back,
in the foreground a mandrel lathe turned by a boy.
It is late afternoon, and the copper light leaking in

from the street side of the shop just catches
his elbow, calf, shoe. Taverns begin to crowd
with workmen curling over their tankards,
still hearing in the rattle of carriages over cobblestone
the steady tap of the treadle,
the gasp and heave of the bellows.

The boy leaves the shop, cringing into the light,
and digs the grime from his fingernails, blue
from bruises. Walking home, he hears a clavier—
Couperin, maybe, a Bach toccata—from a window overhead.
Music, he thinks, *the beautiful.*
Tavern doors open. Voices. Grab and hustle of the street.
Cart wheels. The small room of his life. The darkening sky.

I listen to the clunk-and-slide of the milling machine,
Maudslay's art of clarity and precision: sculpture of poppet,
saddle, jack screw, pawl, cone-pulley,
the fit and mesh of gears, tooth in groove like interlaced fingers.
I think of Mozart folding and unfolding his napkin
as the notes sound in his head. The new machinist sings Patsy Cline,
"I Fall to Pieces." Sparrows bicker overhead.
Screed of the grinder, the band saw's groan and wail.

In his boredom the boy in Diderot
studies again through the shop's open door

the buttresses of Suger's cathedral
and imagines the young Leonardo in his apprenticeship
staring through the window at Brunelleschi's dome,
solid yet miraculous, a resurrected body, floating above the city.

Outside, a cowbird cries, flapping up from the pipe rack,
the ruffling of wings like a quilt flung over a bed.
Snow settles on the tops of cans, black rings in a white field.
The stock, cut clean, gleams under lamplight.
After work, I wade back through the silence of the shop:
the lathes shut down, inert, like enormous animals in hibernation,
red oil rags lying limp on the shoulders
of machines, dust motes still climbing shafts
of dawn light, hook and hoist chain lying desultory
as an old drunk collapsed outside a bar,
barn sparrows pecking on the shores of oil puddles—
emptiness, wholeness; a cave, a cathedral.

As morning light washes the walls of Florence,
the boy Leonardo mixes paints in Verrocchio's shop
and watches the new apprentice muddle
the simple task of the Madonna's shawl.
Leonardo whistles a *canzone* and imagines
a lathe: the spindle, bit, and treadle, the gleam of brass.

FROM

Early Occult Memory Systems of the Lower Midwest

(2003)

On the rough wet grass of the back yard my father and mother have spread quilts. We all lie there, my mother, my father, my uncle, my aunt, and I too am lying there. First we were sitting up, then one of us lay down, and then we all lay down, on our stomachs, or on our sides, or on our backs, and they have kept on talking. They are not talking much, and the talk is quiet, of nothing in particular, of nothing at all in particular, of nothing at all. The stars are wide and alive, they seem each like a smile of great sweetness, and they seem very near. All my people are larger bodies than mine, quiet, with voices gentle and meaningless like the voices of sleeping birds. . . . By some chance, here they are, all on this earth; and who shall ever tell the sorrow of being on this earth, lying, on quilts, on the grass, in a summer evening, among the sounds of the night. May god bless my people, my uncle, my aunt, my mother, my good father, oh, remember them kindly in their time of trouble; and in the hour of their taking away.

After a little I am taken in and put to bed. Sleep, soft smiling, draws me unto her: and those receive me, who quietly treat me, as one familiar and well-beloved in that home: but will not, oh, will not, not now, not ever; but will not ever tell me who I am.

—JAMES AGEE, *A DEATH IN THE FAMILY*

Early Occult Memory Systems
of the Lower Midwest

In his fifth year the son, deep in the backseat
of his father's Ford and the *mysterium*
of time, holds time in memory with words,
night, this night, on the way to a stalled rig south
of Kiowa Creek where the plains wind stacks
the skeletons of weeds on barbed-wire fences
and rattles the battered DeKalb sign to make
the child think of time in its passing, of death.

Cattle stare at flat-bed haulers gunning clumps
of black smoke and lugging damaged drill pipe
up the gullied, mud-hollowed road. *Road, this
road.* Roustabouts shouting from the crow's nest
float like Ascension angels on a ring of lights.
Chokecherries gouge the purpled sky, cloud-
swags running the moon under, and starlight
rains across the Ford's blue hood. *Blue, this blue.*

Later, where black flies haunt the mud tank,
the boy walks along the pipe rack dragging
a stick across the hollow ends to make a kind
of music, and the creek throbs with frog songs,
locusts, the rasp of tree limbs blown and scattered.
The great horse people, his father, these sounds,
these shapes saved from time's dark creek as the car
moves across the moving earth: *world, this world.*

Moses Yellowhorse Is Throwing Water Balloons from the Hotel Roosevelt

The combed lawn of the Villa Carlotta
cools the bare feet of my aesthetic friend
cooing *Beautiful, so beautiful, a dream* . . .
beneath the fat leaves of catalpa trees,
and my Marxist friend—ironic, mordant—
groans, *Ah, yes, indeed, how beautifully*
the rich lie down upon the backs of the poor,
but I am somewhere else, an empty field
near Black Bear Creek in western Oklahoma,
brought there by that ancient word, *dream,*
my father saying, *You had the dream, Horse,*
and two men toss a baseball back and forth
as the sun dissolves behind the pearl-gray strands
of a cirrus and the frayed, flaming branches
along the creek so that the men, too, seem
to be on fire, and the other one, a tall Pawnee
named Moses Yellowhorse, drops his glove,
But I wasn't a man there, and *there,* I know,
is Pittsburgh, and *man* means something more
like *human,* for as a boy I had heard
this story many times, beginning, always,
He was the fastest I ever caught—the fastest,
I think, there ever was, and I was stunned
because for a boy in America, to be the *fastest*
was to be a god, and now my father
and his brothers move behind a scrim

of dust in a fallow wheat field, a blanket
stretched between two posts to make a backstop,
stand of maize to mark the outfield wall,
while their father watches, *If an Indian*
can make it, then so by God can they,
and so it goes, this story of failure
in America: Icarus unwarned,
strapped with his father's wings, my father
one winter morning patching the drive line
of an old Ford tractor with a strand
of baling wire, blood popping out along
his knuckles, and then in fury turning
to his father, *I'm not good enough,*
I'll never get there, and I'm sorry,
I'm goddamned sorry, while Moses Yellowhorse
is drunk again and throwing water balloons
from the Hotel Roosevelt because now
he is "Chief" Yellowhorse, and even though
in a feat of almost *angelic* beauty
he struck out Gehrig, Ruth, and Lazzeri
with nine straight heaters, something isn't right,
so one day he throws a headball at Ty Cobb,
then tells my father, *He was an Indian-hater,*
even his teammates smiled, and now, trying
to explain this to my friends, it occurs to me
that, unlike the Villa Carlotta, baseball is

a question of neither beauty nor politics
but rather mythology, the collective dream,
the old dream, of men becoming gods
or at the very least, as they remove
their wings, being recognized as men.

Mrs. Hill

I am so young that I am still in love
with Battle Creek, Michigan: decoder rings,
submarines powered by baking soda,
whistles that only dogs can hear. Actually,
not even them. Nobody can hear them.

Mrs. Hill from next door is hammering
on our front door shouting, and my father
in his black and gold gangster robe lets her in
trembling and bunched up like a rabbit in snow
pleading, *oh I'm so sorry, so sorry,*
so sorry, and clutching the neck of her gown
as if she wants to choke herself. *He said*
he was going to shoot me. He has a shotgun
and he said he was going to shoot me.

I have never heard of such a thing. A man
wanting to shoot his wife. His wife.
I am standing in the center of a room
barefoot on the cold linoleum, and a woman
is crying and being held and soothed
by my mother. Outside, through the open door
my father is holding a shotgun,
and his shadow envelops Mr. Hill,
who bows his head and sobs into his hands.

A line of shadows seems to be moving
across our white fence: hunched-over soldiers
on a death march, or kindly old ladies
in flower hats lugging grocery bags.

At Roman's Salvage tire tubes
are hanging from trees, where we threw them.
In the corner window of Beacon Hardware there's a sign:
WHO HAS 3 OR 4 ROOMS FOR ME. SPEAK NOW.
For some reason Mrs. Hill is wearing mittens.
Closed in a fist, they look like giant raisins.
In the *Britannica Junior Encyclopaedia*
the great Pharoahs are lying in their tombs,
the library of Alexandria is burning.
Somewhere in Cleveland or Kansas City
the Purple Heart my father refused in WWII
is sitting in a Muriel cigar box,
and every V-Day someone named Schwartz
or Jackson gets drunk and takes it out.

In the kitchen now Mrs. Hill is playing
gin rummy with my mother and laughing
in those long shrieks that women have
that make you think they are dying.

I walk into the front yard where moonlight
drips from the fenders of our Pontiac Chieftain.
I take out my dog whistle. Nothing moves.
No one can hear it. Dogs are asleep all over town.

The Potato Eaters

They are gathered there, as I recall, in the descending light
of Kansas autumn—the welder, the machinist, the foreman,
the apprentice—with their homemade dinners
in brown sacks lying before them on the broken rotary table.
The shop lights have not yet come on. The sun ruffling
the horizon of wheat fields lifts their gigantic shadows
up over the lathes that stand momentarily still and immense,

sleeping gray animals released from the turmoil,
the grind of iron and steel, these past two days.
There is something in the droop of the men's sleeves
and heavy underwater movements of their arms and hands
that suggests they are a dream and I am the dreamer,
even though I am there, too. I have just delivered the dinners
and wait in a pool of shadows, unsure of what to do next.

They unwrap the potatoes from the aluminum foil
with an odd delicacy, and I notice their still blackened hands
as they halve and butter them. The coffee sends up steam
like lathe smoke, and their bodies slowly relax
as they give themselves to the pleasure of the food
and the shop's strange silence after hours of noise,
the clang of iron and the burst and hiss of the cutting torch.

Without looking up, the machinist says something
to anyone who will listen, says it into the great cave

of the darkening shop, and I hear the words, *life,*
my life. I am a boy, so I do not know true weariness,
but I can sense what these words mean, these gestures,
when I stare at the half-eaten potatoes, the men,
the shadows that will pale and vanish as the lights come on.

Hearing Parker the First Time

The blue notes spiraling up from the transistor radio
tuned to WNOE, New Orleans, lifted me out of bed
in Seward County, Kansas, where the plains wind riffed
telephone wires in tones less strange than the bird songs

of Charlie Parker. I played high school tenor sax the way,
I thought, Coleman Hawkins and Lester Young might have
if they were, like me, untalented and white, but "Ornithology"
came winding up from the dark delta of blues and Dixieland

into my room on the treeless and hymn-ridden high plains
like a dust devil spinning me into the Eleusinian Mysteries
of the jazz gods though later I would learn that his long
apprenticeship in Kansas City and an eremite's devotion

to the hard rule of craft gave him the hands that held
the reins of the white horse that carried him to New York
and 52nd Street, farther from wheat fields and dry creek beds
than I would ever travel, and then carried him away.

Delivering Eggs to the Girls' Dorm

> I am the eggman, . . .
>
> —JOHN LENNON

For me it was the cherry blossoms flooding
Olive Street and softening the dawn,
the windows flung open in a yawn,
billowing curtains pregnant with the breeze,
the sounds of Procul Harum entering the air,
and fifty girls rising in their underwear.

O lost love. My girl and I had just split up.
The leaves of chestnut trees were rinsed in black,
the wind moaned grief, the moon was on the rack.
Humped over, stacking egg crates in my Ford,
I was Charles Laughton ringing bells at Notre Dame—
spurned, wounded, but still in love with Sheila Baum.

Arriving at the gates of paradise,
I rang the service bell to wait on
Mrs. Cornish in her saintly apron
fumbling at the door, and the raucous gush
of female voices when she opened it. The flour
in her beard announced the darkness of the hour:

You're late. The hiss of bacon, pancake batter
as it kissed the grill, were a swarm of snakes to warn
the innocent away. Inside were virgins born,
like Sheila Baum, to stay that way. Outside

stood the egg man, despairing in his oval fate:
fifty girls staring, eggless, at an empty plate.

They may still be staring there. For emptiness
became my theme, sweeping eggshells
from my car, driving empty streets, fall's
cherry trees as bare as dormitory walls
washed by September rains. And the bells of Notre Dame
were as still as the broken shell of my dream of Sheila Baum.

Rave On

. . . Wild to be wreckage forever.

—JAMES DICKEY, "CHERRYLOG ROAD"

Rumbling over caliche with a busted muffler,
radio blasting Buddy Holly over Baptist wheat fields,
Travis screaming out *Prepare ye the way of the Lord*
at jackrabbits skittering beneath our headlights,
the Messiah coming to Kansas in a flat-head Ford
with bad plates, the whole high plains holding its breath,
night is fast upon us, lo, in these the days of our youth,
and we were hell on wheels or thought we were. Boredom
grows thick as maize in Kansas, heavy as drill pipe
littering the racks of oil rigs where in summer boys
roustabout or work on combine crews north as far
as Canada. The ones left back in town begin
to die, dragging Main Street shit-faced on 3.2 beer
and banging on the whorehouse door in Garden City
where the ancient madam laughed and turned us down
since we were only boys and she knew our fathers.
We sat out front spitting Red Man and scanned a landscape
flat as Dresden: me, Mike Luckinbill, Billy Heinz,
and Travis Doyle, who sang, *I'm gonna live fast,*
love hard, and die young. We had eaten all the life
there was in Seward County but hungry still, hauled ass
to old Arkalon, the ghost town on the Cimarron
that lay in half-shadow and a scattering of starlight,
and its stillness was a kind of death, the last breath

of whatever in our lives was ending. We had drunk there
and tossed our bottles at the walls and pissed great arcs
into the Kansas earth where the dust groweth hard
and the clods cleave fast together, yea, where night yawns
above the river in its long, dark dream, above
haggard branches of mesquite, chicken hawks scudding
into the tree line, and moon-glitter on caliche
like the silver plates of Coronado's treasure
buried all these years, but the absence of treasure,
absence of whatever would return the world
to the strangeness that as children we embraced
and recognized as *life*. *Rave on*.
                                    Cars are cheap
at Roman's Salvage strewn along the fence out back
where cattle graze and chew rotting fabric from the seats.
Twenty bucks for spare parts and a night in the garage
could make them run as far as death and stupidity
required—on Johnson Road where two miles of low shoulders
and no fence line would take you up to sixty, say,
and when you flipped the wheel clockwise, you were there
rolling in the belly of the whale, belly of hell,
and your soul fainteth within you for we had seen it done
by big Ed Ravenscroft who said you would go in a boy
and come out a man, and so we headed back through town
where the marquee of the Plaza flashed CREATURE FROM
THE BLACK LAGOON in storefront windows and the Snack Shack

where we had spent our lives was shutting down and we
sang *rave on, it's a crazy feeling* out into the night
that loomed now like a darkened church, and sang loud
and louder still for we were sore afraid.
                                       Coming up
out of the long tunnel of cottonwoods that opens onto
Johnson Road, Travis with his foot stuck deep into the *soul*
of that old Ford *come on, Bubba, come on* beating
the dash with his fist, hair flaming back in the wind
and eyes lit up by some fire in his head that I
had never seen, and Mike, iron Mike, sitting tall
in back with Billy, who would pick a fight with anything
that moved but now hunched over mumbling something
like a prayer, as the Ford lurched on spitting
and coughing but then smoothing out suddenly fast
and the fence line quitting so it was open field, then,
then, I think, we were butt-deep in regret and a rush
of remembering whatever we would leave behind—
Samantha Dobbins smelling like fresh laundry,
light from the movie spilling down her long blonde hair,
trout leaping all silver and pink from Black Bear Creek,
the hand of my mother, I confess, passing gentle
across my face at night when I was a child—oh, yes,
it was all good now and too late, trees blurring
past and Travis wild, popping the wheel, oh too late
too late

and the waters pass over us the air thick
as mud slams against our chest though turning now
the car in its slow turning seems almost graceful
the frame in agony like some huge animal groaning
and when the wheels leave the ground the engine cuts loose
with a wail thin and ragged as a band saw cutting tin
and we are drowning breathless heads jammed against
our knees and it's a thick swirling purple nightmare
we cannot wake up from for the world is turning too
and I hear Billy screaming and then the whomp
sick crunch of glass and metal whomp *again back window*
popping loose and glass exploding someone crying out
tink tink *of iron on iron overhead and then at last*
it's over and the quiet comes

                            Oh so quiet. Somewhere
the creak and grind of a pumping unit. Crickets.
The tall grass sifting the wind in a mass of whispers
that I know I'll be hearing when I die. And so
we crawled trembling from doors and windows borne out
of rage and boredom into weed-choked fields barren
as Golgotha. Blood raked the side of Travis's face
grinning rapt, ecstatic, Mike's arm was hanging down
like a broken curtain rod, Billy kneeled, stunned,
listening as we all did to the rustling silence
and the spinning wheels in their sad, manic song

as the Ford's high beams hurled their crossed poles of light
forever out into the deep and future darkness. *Rave on.*

I survived. We all did. And then came the long surrender,
the long, slow drifting down like young hawks riding on
the purest, thinnest air, the very palm of God
holding them aloft so close to something hidden there,
and then the letting go, the fluttering descent, claws
spread wide against the world, and we become, at last,
our fathers. And do not know ourselves and therefore
no longer know each other. Mike Luckinbill ran a Texaco
in town for years. Billy Heinz survived a cruel divorce,
remarried, then took to drink. But finally last week
I found this house in Arizona where the brothers
take new names and keep a vow of silence and make
a quiet place for any weary, or lost, passenger
of earth whose unquiet life has brought him there,
and so, after vespers, I sat across the table
from men who had not surrendered to the world,
and one of them looked at me and looked into me,
and I am telling you there was *a fire in his head*
and his eyes were coming fast down a caliche road,
and I knew this man, and his name was Travis Doyle.

A Photograph of the *Titanic*

When Travis came home from the monastery,
the ground had vanished beneath him,
and he went everywhere in bare feet

as if he were walking on a plane of light,
and he spoke of his sleepless nights
and of a picture in *National Geographic:*

a pair of shoes from the *Titanic* resting
on the ocean floor. They were blue
against a blue ground and a black garden

of iron and brass. The toes pointed outward,
toward two continents, and what had been
inside them had vanished so completely

that he imagined it still there, with the sea's
undersway bellying down each night
as each day after compline he fell into

his bed, the dark invisible bulk of tons
pushing down on the shoes, nudging them
across the blue floor, tossing them aside

like a child's hands in feverish sleep
until the shoestrings scattered and dissolved.
Sometimes he would dream of the shoes

coming to rest where it is darkest,
after the long fall before we are born,
when we gather our bodies around us,

when we curl into ourselves and drift
toward the little sleep we have rehearsed
again and again as if falling we might drown.

Blood Rain

Beset by an outbreak of plague in 1503, Nurembergers were
further terrified by a concurrent phenomenon called a blood rain,
. . . Dürer recorded the resulting stains on a servant girl's linen
shift: . . . a crucifix flanked by ghostly figures.

—FRANCES RUSSELL, *THE WORLD OF DÜRER 1471–1528.*

Like rust on iron, red algae invading rain.
And again, the plague. Nuremberg in ruin.
At home alone, the artist prays for grace
while, gates flung open, the neighbor's geese
roam the yard in droves, and their wild honks
and the ravings of a servant girl bring Dürer
to the window. She stands there, her wet hair
clumped in black strands, and her arms fall limp
in a great sob, her head lolling, while the damp
shift she wears blotters the rain in red streaks—
like wounds slowly spreading, Dürer sees, *to make
a sign:* in the bleeding fabric of her dress
as if etched in copper hangs Christ upon His Cross
between two ghosts. Cruel miracles, God's grace
drawn in God's blood on the body of a girl who sighs
at him, swoons, and collapses in the mud.

Outside, gutters turning scarlet, the dead
hauled from house to wagon, cries of women
battering the windowpanes. Inside, the burin
drops from Dürer's hand as the girl wakes
and rises from the bench below his portrait,
done in Munich the year of the apocalypse, but

never to be sold, never to leave the artist's house.
She touches once more God's message on her dress,
then turns and stares at the painting's face
so solemn, so godlike in its limpid gaze,
that she backs away to study the long brown locks
spread evenly about His shoulders, the beatific
right hand held more gently than the blessing
of a priest, and the inscription in a tongue
she does not understand. *This is Christ!*
No, it's me, he says, touching hand to chest,

the rough right hand, the human chest, the heart's dream
of art's divinity as death rolls down the street.

The Death of a Psychic

The obituary in the L.A. *Times* says that you foresaw
your own death, also a boy, dead, in a storm drain
with the wrong shoes on the wrong feet. Death
became your specialty: a yellow shirt, the flung

corsage near, vaguely, water, the odd detail drawing
squad cars and ambulance to the scene you dreaded.
I imagine nightmares that you woke up to instead
of from, the heavy winter coat of prophecy that hung

from your shoulders any season, especially summer
when mayhem bloomed below a bleeding sun
and dark angels, gorged on smog and heat, unfurled
their wings to wake you gasping in your dampened bed,

again, once more. No theophanies, no "still small voice"
or hovering dove, but only gray, murky hunches
bubbling from the mud of intuition, the sudden starts
and flights of vision, and of course, its shadow, fear.

But to live haunted by the knowledge of a certain year
when you would stumble in your flannel house robe
through a sunlit kitchen and lie down on cold linoleum
beneath, at last, the wide wings of the present tense.

Luck

I sit looking into the mirror at the bitter man
sitting opposite me whose book has been rejected
for the last time: the familiar face I have never liked,
the mournful eyes, mournful even in happiness,
broken mouth, nose like a fig, the melancholy face
of a man whose gift of perseverance I have admired
though now he disappoints me as I watch
the blue bile of self-pity welling up in drab,
sad little lunettes below his eyes. I begin to think,
I am lucky, I am lucky, to live in a country
where the son of a machinist can piss away his time
writing poems, . . . and I think of that odd word,
lucky, its strange sound, the *uck* sound
of a duck barfing or even choking to death,
its ridiculous webbed feet fanning the air,
writhing *uck, uck,* or the miserable, queer sound
of galoshes unstuck from the mud, *uck,* the sound
of disgust at the vile, sick, nasty, repugnant,
the blackened lemon stuck under the fruit bin, *uck,*
the gross, the foul, the *lucky,* rhyming with FUCK E
as in Fuck Everett written in dust on the back
of a semi hauling dog food to Peoria or painted
in Day-Glo on the water tower by E's acne-ridden,
rabid ex-girlfriend, but there is, on the other hand,
lucky's lovely "L" sound, preferred by Yeats
among all phonemes, called a *liquid* and cited

in all the Intro. to Poetry texts for its melody,
its grace, its small-breasted, skinny-hipped, lithe
evocativeness, "L," the Audrey Hepburn of consonants,
as in *lily, ladle, lap, lip, lust, labia, loquacious,*
or LUCKY!, e.g., *Hail! Good fortune attend thee,*
Horatio, you lucky bastard, or *Good luck, Leonard,*
I hope you get lucky, or the word being implicit
in the deed, therefore the very act, the event, of luck,
the sun coming out in the fifth inning, a ten-dollar bill
falling out of the dryer, the tragic diagnosis reversed,
Jules and Jim and *One-Eyed Jacks* back-to-back,
no school, a cool summer, a warm winter, the big,
beautiful book containing twenty years of poems
WITH YOUR NAME ON THEM, *lucky,* a stupid word,
a wrong word, easily used, badly understood, the tiny,
pathetic wet dream of me and Everett and that whole town
surrounding a water tower where a girl stands
with phosphorescent green paint dribbling down
her wrist, mumbling, *luck, oh luck, just a little, just some, luck.*

A Roman Grave

He begins to fear the gray morning light,
the absence out of which each day arises,
an iron sun dragging through a grinding fog.

Along the mews the long cars of the Romanovs
move quietly as clouds to line the curb
of the Russian Orthodox Church in Exile.

He sees them far below as crows, black umbrellas
slick with rain beneath the red-leaved trees,
old women draped in veils and funeral scarves.

A Europe of confusions, history's scattered
flocks mumbling unintelligible prayers
while the chauffeurs take out their cigarettes.

Later, he watches diggers on the Thames'
south side haul up rocks from a Roman grave,
a girl buried beside her brother. Strata

lie piled like quilts beside the small pits
where a man and woman kneel in their shadows.
The dead in their stone sleep are roused into

history. The living pray into the earth and wait.

On the Passing of Jesus Freaks
from the College Classroom

They seemed to come in armies, whole platoons
uniformed in headbands, cut-off jeans,
butt-long hair that fell down in festoons,
and their grins were the ends that justified the means.

But one was different. And alone. His wrist tattoo
cried FATHER on a severed heart that bled.
His arms hung limp as vines, his nails were blue,
his silence was the chorus of the dead.

"Are you saved?" they asked. "Saved from what," I said.
"The flames of hell, your rotten, sinful past,
your thing for Desdemona," for we had read
the tragedies, and *Othello* was the last.

"What's Iago's motive? Was he just *sinful*?"
They thought they knew but waited for a hint.
He raised his hands and wept, "Evil, fucking Evil."
And he meant it. *And he knew what he meant.*

Brazil

This is for Elton Wayne Showalter, redneck surrealist
who, drunk, one Friday night tried to hold up the local 7-Eleven
with a caulking gun, and who, when Melinda Bozell boasted
that she would never let a boy touch her "down there," said,
"Down there? You mean, like, Brazil?"

Oh, Elton Wayne,
with your silver-toed turquoise-on-black boots and Ford Fairlane
dragging, in a ribbon of sparks, its tailpipe down Main Street
Saturday nights, you dreamed of Brazil and other verdant lands,
but the southern hemisphere remained for all those desert years
a vast mirage shimmering on the horizon of what one might call
your mind, following that one ugly night at the Snack Shack
when, drunk again, you peed on your steaming radiator
to cool it down and awoke at the hospital, groin empurpled
from electric shock and your pathetic maleness swollen
like a bruised tomato. You dumb bastard, betting a week's wages
on the trifecta at Raton, then in ecstasy tossing the winning
ticket into the air and watching it float on an ascending breeze
out over the New Mexico landscape forever and beyond: gone.
The tears came down, but the spirit rose late on Sunday night
on a stepladder knocking the middle letters from FREEMAN GLASS
to announce unlimited sexual opportunities in purple neon
for all your friends driving Kansas Avenue as we did each night
lonely and boredom-racked and hungering for someone like you,
Elton Wayne, brilliantly at war in that flat, treeless county
against maturity, right-thinking, and indeed intelligence

in all its bland, local guises, so that now reading the announcement
in the hometown paper of your late marriage to Melinda Bozell
with a brief honeymoon at the Best Western in Junction City,
I know that you have finally arrived, in Brazil, and the Kansas
that surrounds you is an endless sea of possibility, genius, love.

Weather Report

We will have a continuation of today tomorrow.

Clouds will form those ragged gloves
in which the hands of God make giant fists
as He grits His teeth against the slaves
of time. And the sun and moon will never rest

from the boring grind of dark and light:
subway tokens glittering the ground,
dogs in their habits, the hours soon or late,
nuns and assassins in their daily round.

The divorcée coming from the laundromat
knows the cycles of laundry and despair:
back then, the towels they shared, but now a basket
filled with someone else's underwear.

Eichmann lies in bed and reads a novel;
a Holocaust survivor sets himself on fire.
The thief's in church, the priest is in the brothel;
the sky is clear, the weatherman's a liar.

God shakes His fists eternally to say,
we're having more of yesterday today.

The Second Annual *Wizard of Oz* Reunion in Liberal, Kansas

They have come once more, the small ones.
They crowd around my mother and her friends
at the F. Nightingale Retirement Home
and sing *Wizard of Oz* songs like hymns

and let themselves be called "munchkins"
by the palsied, ancient ones who cling
to that memory and Dorothy taken
through the Kansas air but cannot recall

the green city or the yellow road that leads there.
Mrs. Beaudry, who owned the coffee shop,
cannot find her hands, and Mr. MacIntyre
is searching for his long-dead wife and is happy,

finally, when she calls. For these the actors
sing their tunes, and for the wheelchair aged
and the ones on metal walkers that clump
like awkward giants through the halls.

For these the rayon flowers, and the Bible
opened to a text they cannot read. For these
a trip to Oz Land, and a photo sent
with a letter in which my mother writes,

Some children came today. They seemed so grown
and fine and reminded me of you back when.
This, to a man with neither courage, brain,
nor heart to find his way back home again.

The Blue Buick

I read the Classics in an English edition; but I would also relax by
unrolling a map of the sky on a big table and covering each
constellation with precious stones from our coffers, marking the
largest stars with the most beautiful diamonds, finishing out these
designs with the most colorful gems, filling the spaces between
with a stream of the most beautiful pearls from Léouba's collection,
. . . They were all beautiful! And I recited to myself that immortal,
and for me unforgettable, page by Marbode on the symbolism of
precious stones which I had just discovered in *Le Latin mystique* by
Rémy de Gourmont, a gem of a book, a compilation, a translation,
an anthology, which turned me upside-down and, in short, baptized
me, or at the very least, converted me to Poetry, initiated me into
the Word, catechized me.

—BLAISE CENDRARS, "LA CHAMBER NOIR DE
L'IMAGINATION," IN *LE LOTISSEMENT DU CIEL*

My imagination goes some years backward, and I remember a beautiful
young girl singing at the edge of the sea in Normandy words and music
of her own composition. She thought herself alone, stood barefooted
between sea and sand; sang with lifted head of the civilisations that
there had come and gone, ending every verse with the cry:
      "O Lord, let something remain"

—WILLIAM BUTLER YEATS, *A VISION*

A boy standing on a rig deck looks across the plains.
A woman walks from a trailer to watch the setting sun.
A man stands beside a lathe, lighting a cigar.
Imagined or remembered, a girl in Normandy
sings across a sea, *that something may remain:*

A blue Buick Dynaflow, sleek, fat, grand, useless
for dragging Main, gunning off the stoplight sluggish

as a cow, but on the highway light and smooth as flight,
the Louvre's *Winged Samothrace* that Roy kept
a postcard of above his lathe, for he had been
to Paris, where he first met his wife, Maria.
I knew him those last years in Kansas before
they left for California, from the summer
of the last great dust storm when I crawled home from school
because I could not see the sidewalk beneath my feet,
the silence hanging, too, in air, the whole town drowning
under dust like Pompeii or Herculaneum,
and I imagined its history now left to me,
and I could tell, then, of the loneliness that fell
across the plains, across the town, looking out
on bald horizons undisturbed by tree lines,
and the gunmetal gray of winter sky brutal
in its placid, constant stare, like the hit man
in *Macbeth, let it come down,* and if there is an Eye
of God, the seer and the seen, it is that sky:
vast, merciless, and bored. Too bored to tell again
the old story of housewives gone mad, farmers standing
alone by the back fence of the back forty weeping
in desperation, the Mexican girl walking nude
out of a wheat field and offering herself
to an entire rig crew for a dollar each, boys
outside the Haymow Club beating each other
unconscious for nothing better to do . . .

The music: an old Reinhardt and Grappelli record
that Roy and Maria brought from Paris,
the sweet, frail voice of an unknown woman
singing "Don't Worry 'Bout Me." It hovers over
and around them, aurora-like, the frayed light
of a blanched photograph, it pursues them always
and everywhere, sailing down Highway 54
in that big boat under a star-strewn sky, parked
under cottonwoods along the Cimarron River,
watching a late-game home run lift into the lights,
and it was there full-volume when Roy came home
from work and they began to dance, martinis in hand,
and soon you were there in the Hot Club in Paris
rather than a tiny Airstream trailer parked
along the southern outskirts of Liberal, Kansas,
where a boy, amazed, sat at a yellow formica
breakfast table watching something that might be,
he wondered, some form, some rare, lucky version,
of human happiness.
            Happiness. And surely
it was there from the beginning, she a dancer,
he a Rotary scholar from Texas escaping Cambridge
to join the excitement of Paris in the early fifties
where he knew Baldwin, even the old man Cendrars,
hung out at jazz clubs along boulevard Saint Germain,
and wrote for two years before returning home

and a season with the Class A Lubbock Hubbers.
After that, seven failed years in Hollywood
(failed, though he would quote with pride the lines he wrote
for Trumbo's *Lonely Are the Brave*), then vanishing
in the oil fields of Bakersfield, trying still to write,
lugging a trailer full of books and landing, finally,
in southwest Kansas in a machine shop managed
by my father, where Roy believed that he was
on the *edge* of something, something *rare*, something more,
even, than Paris, though to my mind it was just
the northern edge of the Oklahoma Panhandle,
known as No Man's Land in the days when horse thieves
and rustlers called it home, and what Roy found there
I still try to understand. Absence. Mystery.
Roy worshiped it, called it *negative capability*
and quoted Keats, said in poetry and lathework,
both arts of precision, it was what lay beyond
the *mot juste,* the closest tolerance, the finest cut,
it was where it all, finally, ended.
                                        Roy Garcia
was the only man my father hired again
after he showed up drunk. *Because he's brilliant,*
the best machinist I've ever seen, and he had seen
a few. *And he's an educated man,* he said,
with that distant, almost spiritual admiration
of someone who had never finished high school.

And he has a good excuse. He meant of course
the seizures, which came on rarely but each time
seemed to happen twice, for Roy would turn to drink—
out of shame, Maria said—and he could handle
one drink, maybe two, but the drunkenness brought on
by shame—not immediate, but lingering, a sense
of being doomed or damned, as if he blamed himself—
would cause another seizure, and Maria
and my father would have to treat him like a child:
confine him to his trailer, put him back on
Tegretol, and make him pull himself together
before he came back on the job. But with "good excuse,"
I knew my father, too, was thinking of his brother,
Mike, who had the same disease. And so he made me
Roy's apprentice, to learn from him but also
to look out for him. Roy could tell when one
was coming on—a void, a tension, in his stomach—
and would lie down on the wooden ramp beside his lathe,
and I would shout for help, someone to keep him
from swallowing his tongue. The *shame* of it, she said,
but if there was shame, there was the other thing as well,
the brief spell before the fit came on that made it
all, he said, almost worthwhile: the rush of light,
his body looking down upon his other body.
At college later, reading Brutus's line, *He hath*

the falling sickness, I would think of this
and wonder: the going hence, the coming hither,
all of it, a confusion and a mystery in those days.

From Roy's Journal: *The marriage of heaven and hell. If the aura is a*
state of grace, then what is the seizure? If in the aura I lose my body,
what do I lose in the other? The old woman on the steps of St. Eustache
weeping, terrified that she had lost her soul.

About one thing, though, I can be exact: that Buick,
baby blue with a white ragtop, double-wide
white sidewalls and about two tons of chrome grillwork
navigating Main Street all fat-assed, gas-guzzling,
and antienvironmental as they come. A dream,
I thought, a big blue dream that summer driving back
from Amarillo with my girl nuzzling against me
and Roy and Maria in the backseat singing
"Crazy" or "I Fall to Pieces" into the stars,
and sometimes on a familiar stretch of blacktop
with no curves or dips and a moon to light the way,
the cathedral dome of night sky turned upside-down
in the blue laminations of the hood, I would
turn off the headlights for a while and fly miles
and miles from earth, more alone and yet not alone
than I have ever been, and just as we reached home,

crossing No Man's Land, the rim of the world would begin
to blaze, and with the rising sun we would drift slowly
back to earth, back to Kansas.

                      Since Paris, Roy
and Maria had been apart just once, when he ran off
to Bakersfield and she chose to stay behind, working
in L.A. with Bronislava Nijinska at her studio
in Hollywood, trying hard to breathe new life
into a ballet career that had never grown beyond
the corps of the smallest company in Paris.
Nijinska finally, of course, with a sense of guilt
almost maternal had to make Maria face
reality, but oddly—since they had grown so close,
because Maria was, as Nijinska often said,
the very echo of her famous protégée,
Maria Tallchief, because it was that tragic case
of desire, self-sacrifice, and even talent
devoured by the accident of failure—gave her
the Buick, a gift from a rich patron, as a kind
of tacit consolation. Seeing this as a sign
and wonder—the end of one life, the beginning
of another—Maria then drove straight to Roy
in Bakersfield, and they had been together
ever since. In her L.A. days, while Roy
was reviving dying screenplays, Maria—
like most dancers, I suppose—also dreamed of acting,

and sometimes we would drive to old Arkalon,
the ghost town on the Cimarron, and there among
the ruins, broken walls, and traces of foundations,
while we drank Pearl beer from quart bottles and gazed
at scraps of night sky sliding down the contours
of the car, she recited lines from parts that she
had *almost* won: Blanche Dubois, or Laura
from *Glass Menagerie,* and Roy would lean back
and look up into the trees and dark beyond, watching
smoke from his cigar rise like small dirigibles
that bore the words of a once aspiring actress
and almost famous dancer named Maria Patterson.

What did I know? I was a blank slate—a phrase,
by the way, I only learned from Roy (read Locke,
then Blake)—and all I knew is that I had to *know.*
To know, in a town with a one-room storefront
library where Durant's *The Story of Philosophy*
was the raft I was floating on, though slowly sinking,
too, in an endless cycle of work/eat/sleep, haunting
the only bookstore within two hundred miles
in Amarillo, when I could get there, and watching
cars pass through to exotic California
with those bright orange plates that seemed to say, *life
is somewhere else.* Sometimes I would drive aimlessly
through No Man's Land, and if I stopped at a little town

called Slapout and asked the lady at the Quick Stop
for the population, she would say, *Seven,*
but the eighth is on its way, and point to her belly.
For God's sake.
                           There were, on the other hand, the movies.
I remember one, especially: *The Country Girl.*
Grace Kelly played the wife of an ex-Broadway star,
an aging alcoholic who's been out of work
but straight for years. The director, William Holden,
needs him badly for his new play, and when he visits
their little drab apartment, Kelly talks across
an ironing board where clothes are piled, her graying hair
lies lank and damp against her neck, but books fill the room,
and Holden picks one up: *Montaigne, I find him*
too polite. Wonderful, I thought, stupidly,
but then Holden understands, these books are *hers,*
and he begins to see that she's the strong one here,
the wise one, she's the one to pull her husband up.
And I saw it, too, or rather saw Grace Kelly,
golden, rising like Athena in a field of books
to make her husband rise, reborn, as an actor
once again, and of course Holden falls in love with her,
but she in turn then falls in love with the new man
she has half-created and *everyone gets exactly*
what they deserve, and walking home that evening

with a half-moon lifting over the machine shop
where I had just spent one more day, I thought
in my pathetic, redneck way, *That must be what folks
call "art."*

Art. What did I know? Nothing, until
Roy and Maria came to town. *Enough Grappelli,*
she would say, and put on a symphony, Mozart,
maybe, or Dvořák's *New World,* which made me
swallow hard and turn my face away because, well,
it was *beautiful,* a word I wasn't easy with back then,
and because, I know now, it seemed to be about the plains
which in their endless silence had no music until
that moment, when I saw my father, his four brothers,
a scrabble farm and three-room house against an empty
landscape and barren future. Sometimes, returning from
a drive to nowhere in particular, she sang fragments
of "Caro Nome," and I would think, how strange,
a song like that here, now, among grazing cattle,
barbed wire, mesquite, endless rows of maize,
and pumping units bobbing up and down like insane,
gigantic blackbirds. And stranger still, Roy
might speak grandly into the wind and waiting fields:
> *In my craft or sullen art,*
> *Exercised in the still night*
> *When only the moon rages*

And lovers lie abed
With all their griefs in their arms . . .
or Keats or Shakespeare or the new one by Lowell
he loved, "The Fat Man in the Mirror," from Werfel:
Only a fat man with his beaver on his eye
Only a fat man,
Only a fat man
Bursts the mirror. O, it is not I!
which I never understood, though I do now,
perhaps. So they were teachers, I suppose, though
messengers is more the word, messengers, travelers
from another world—as Eluard said, the world
that is inside this one—and they came bearing
the messages, the anthology, that would change
my life: St. Augustine's *Confessions, The Brothers
Karamazov,* Conrad, *A Little Treasury
of Modern Poetry,* Gombrich's survey, Hart Crane,
Dickinson's *Collected,* Ring Lardner, Salinger,
Flannery O'Connor, a Chekhov story called
"The Student," *Winesburg, Ohio,* Joyce's "The Dead,"
a little book on Kierkegaard by Auden, "The Snows
of Kilimanjaro," a signed copy of Baldwin's
Go Tell It on the Mountain, and what must have been
a first edition of *Let Us Now Praise Famous Men.*
But at the end of the bottom shelf of books that lined

their little trailer was one in French by Blaise Cendrars:
Le Lotissement du ciel (*The Subdividing
of the Sky,* my translation), the strangest book,
Roy said, he ever read by the most intriguing man
he ever knew. Cendrars, the one-armed legend,
veteran of the front in both world wars, citizen
of a dozen countries, friend of Chagall, Léger,
Apollinaire, Modigliani: a man who had read
everything, done everything, and when Roy
knew him still talked endlessly of *Sky*'s main subject:
the levitation of saints in the ecstatic state
called by St. John of the Cross *al arrobamiento
de amor:* the ravishment of love. *Cendrars,
the old surrealist,* Roy would say, *obsessesed
with bodies rising in air when his only son,
the pilot, died by falling to earth.* He came back
to this repeatedly. And to Giordano Bruno,
who Roy said was more important than Galileo,
and he taught me Bruno's memory system,
the nearest thing to immortality, he said,
for then I would forget nothing, and everything
would be imprinted on my soul.

The Journal: *Cendrars in "The Ravishment of Love." "The saint also
has his migraines and his gross lassitude. . . . He is suspicious of*

illusions, dream-somnambulism, the acrobatics of certain drunk
and manic states, and the nervous breakdowns of certain epileptics
and neurotics."

So I remembered
everything, the small as well as large, the photo
of Roy and Robert Rossen in Hollywood
(the screenplay of *Treasure of the Sierra Madre*
with Rossen's name on it), all the stories
that Maria told of Nijinska and her brother,
the trip to Amarillo when Patsy Cline performed,
even the hometown ball games we would go to,
we three on summer evenings when the fragrance
of new mown outfield grass was hanging in the air
and the lights came on to carve the darkening sky
into a big blue bowl. *A ball diamond,* he would say,
is the most aesthetically pure form ever given
to a playing field, and as a student of geometry
I could understand that, the way the diamond fits
inside a circle enclosed within a larger one
extending from the arc along the outfield wall.
And the way the game itself falls into curves:
runners rounding base paths; the arc of the long ball's
sudden rise and floating, slow descent, sometimes
into the outer darkness beyond the left field wall;
the shape a double play can take when the shortstop

snags the ball on his far right and the second baseman
makes a fluid pivot so the ball seems to glide
in an unbroken line around to first; and of course
a killer curve or good knuckle ball by someone like
Preacher Roe or Whitey Ford whose looping arc
briefly mesmerizes the batter it deceives;
all a game of curves and arcs, though Maria
said it was a game of tension, a gathering,
then release, a kind of sexual tension, the way
the pitcher coiled, then unwound, and of course
the explosive letting go, and she said it in a way
that made me stop and think awhile. In a plane once
I saw a diamond far below all lit up,
an emerald resting on the breast of darkness, and now
I recall Maria and the curve from her neck along
the jawline to her raised chin as she followed
the arc of the ball in flight and the way her eyes
gave back the flare of the outfield lights at night.

As with baseball and poetry, so with lathework,
arts of precision: an able catcher sets his feet
to avoid the extra step that makes him miss
the steal at second, a poet hears the syllable
before the word, a good machinist "feels" the cut
before he measures it. These minute distinctions
were Roy's delight, *The Machinist's Handbook*

his guide to prosody. And I tried but somehow
failed the craft—in fact, one time almost ran the bit
into the chuck, unknown to my worried father,
who was losing hope for me: if Roy couldn't teach me,
who could? But my head was in baseball, books, music:
my tenor saxophone and I would someday be
on 52nd Street in New York, where we belonged,
and so I made Roy talk about his father's friend,
the great jazz trumpeter, Roy Eldridge, whose name
he took, and the jazz scene in Paris in the fifties
where Roy and Maria on any given night
could hear Bud Powell, Lester Young, Kenny Clarke,
Dexter Gordon, even Sidney Bechet, even sometimes
the Bird himself, and Maria, smiling, recalled
standing outside The Ringside, later The Blue Note,
one night as Parker's astonishing long riff
on "Green Dolphin Street" rose over the waiting crowd,
over the lamps reflected in the Seine, up and beyond
Haussmann's Paris and the opulent Palais Garnier,
a black man's music rising and hovering over
this pearl of Europe from a small room far below
on the rue d'Artois.
                    Decades later I would walk
this street and others: rue Coquillière,
where Roy met Cendrars, where, I imagined,
he rose finally from the table, feeling the weight,

the burden, of being young and unknown, and strolled
past Saint-Eustache through the jazz-thick air of the clubs
in Les Halles to the little room on rue du Jour
that he shared with Maria, where they drank the last
of their wine and gazed from the balcony toward
the distant future. And whatever they saw there,
it could not have been Liberal, Kansas. What dreams
they must have had! Raising his glass of Chartreuse
after dinner, Roy would sing out the line from Larbaud,
Assez de mots, assez de phrases! ô vie réelle,
and Maria would pull the album from the hope chest
and turn to the photographs, so predictable
they broke your heart: a girl and boy leaning
against the stones of Pont Neuf, the Seine stretching
behind them, the girl small, sharp-boned, bright brown eyes,
a dancer's bun, and you could almost see her thin lips
trembling with the hesitation that sometimes precedes
pure joy, the boy with slicked-back hair, cigarette
dangling from one hand, the other pressing his girl close.
That evening, I remember, Maria was playing
an old 78 of Bidú Sayão singing Massenet,
and for a moment in my eyes they froze, Maria
lost in thought, staring down into the images
as if she wanted to walk into them, Roy
gazing at his glass as if it were a crystal ball
or piece of lathework, finished, done, no turning back.

We were at a rig just south of Tyrone, Oklahoma,
in No Man's Land one day inspecting thread damage
on some battered drill pipe when Roy suddenly
turned away and moved into the shadow of our truck,
head down, almost cowering, the dark wing of anguish
sweeping across his face. *It's the light,* he said.
Fucking treeless Oklahoma. Strong light sometimes
brings it on. He reached into the cab and handed me
some rubber tubing. *I'll stay here in the shade.*
I'll be o.k. But if it comes, put this between my teeth
so I don't bite my tongue. Don't worry, I'll know ahead
of time. I'll warn you. But of course there was no warning
this time as the sun broke behind a cloud and his body
dropped to earth thudding, writhing, shoveling dust
all around as his heels dug in, legs shaking, hands
clawing the ground, and his teeth gnashing so terribly
I could hardly wedge the rubber tube between them.
The St. Christopher was wound around his neck
so tight I had to break its chain, his eyes flaring
and rolling back white as cue balls when the gagging
began its dry sucking sound, that rattle and gasp,
and I knew then that it, the thing, had to be done:
Is there a more intimate gesture than placing one's hand
in the mouth of another man? All I could think
as I groped inside that mess of flesh and wetness
was how we would be seen from the rig's deck: two men,

one writhing in the dirt, the other strangling him
in the last throes of dying, and when it was over
and he lay there breathing fast and staring at the sky,
I thought that I had died, not him, and I rose up
and watched with dead eyes two dust devils in the distance
spinning out across the barren fields of No Man's Land.

The Journal: *Told Maria today. Says it's just too dangerous. But what
the hell else can I do? Terrible, terrible sight for a young kid. This time
on a bridge with Maria, the river is black, sky black, a photographic
negative. That bizarre music again, like* The Isle of the Dead. *The
rising into light, probably only a second, but so slow, Nijinsky, now
there was a man with a fire in his head.* And kingdoms naked in the
trembling heart—Te Deum laudamus O Thou Hand of Fire.

I know how Roy and I must look to you, she said.
We seem like . . . , she tried, *you must think . . .*
Roy passed out on phenobartibal, radio off,
we were driving back from Wichita where our team
had won a tournament that day. Grain elevator,
church spire in the distance, one more small town,
and twenty miles after that, another. A patch
of soybean flung forward by the sweep of headlights,
long shadow of a stand of maize, then nothing
but the night sky slipping like a sequined and slowly
unwinding bolt of black cloth across the Buick's hood,

the earth rolling beneath the rolling car so that,
a child might think, they would return in time and space
to the same point, same field of bending wheat,
DeKalb sign rattling on a fence post, wind sifting
through high grass, moaning on barbed wire—*my life,* I thought.
I knew what she was trying hard to say, and not
to say: failure. *That's how Roy and I must seem to you.*
No, I said, *not at all.* But she wouldn't hear of it,
and so began the litany of failure in America,
wind pushing the tears sideways across her face,
Bright beginnings, yes, I guess, but no grief here,
none. By God, we've made a life, and that's enough:
a life. Listen, Nijinsky went nuts. Bronislava,
a driven woman. All those big-shot émigrés
in Santa Monica trying to believe they were on
vacation in the south of France. What brought us here,
I don't understand. One thing happens. Then another.
We make do. We survive. It's just not that complex.
Oh yes it was. I was seventeen, and I knew.
It was vast, entangled, difficult, profound.
And as we rolled on through the deep sleep of small towns
strewn along the highway, the odd light of a house
like a single unshut eye somewhere on the edge,
the silence of the high plains huge yet imminent,
like the earth's held breath, I knew, it was not here

That's what I mean, stud, Roy would say, *that's my point
exactly. The held breath. As if we haven't quite
begun yet to exist. That coming into being
still going on. That final form just waiting,
the world waiting. And it's not just geography,
though that's part of it. Anderson had a sense of this
in* Winesburg, *those tragic little lives bordering
on something unknown, possible, huge—Dickinson,
too, sitting in her little room, Jesus, the walls
must have vibrated. For God's sake, this is not
the Wasteland, kid. London is. Or Paris.
This place has no history. And if you want to see
the absolute end of the road, try Venice.
You'll fall in love with her, everybody does,
but on the honeymoon you'll find you're crawling
in bed with a corpse. There are people still living
in this town who came up on the Jones and Plummer trail
when the only law was that the strong survived
and the weak didn't, who knew and lived something that
Kropotkin only dreamed: a state of total anarchy.
You know, L.A. was once like this. And then Chandler
and his pals moved in and conspired to do
what Lorenzo de' Medici had planned for Florence
and the Arno: divert a river so that one town
died and another prospered. So L.A. grew*

and became what? A false Florence with faux-European
architecture, fake art (read Nathanael West),
synthetic landscape, and right next door on the coast,
a phony Venice with canals and everything.
And Chandler became the new, improved Medici,
all spiritual possibility gone, bought and sold,
infinities of human imagination
subdivided and air-conditioned. And, of course,
the new politics: metaphysical democracy—
nothing is genuine, everything is equally unreal.
Well, I'd rather be here.
                                And he pulled a book
from the shelf and read again in a too-loud,
prophetic voice those strange lines from Crane's *The Bridge:*

And kingdoms
              naked in the
                              trembling heart—
Te Deum laudamus
              O Thou Hand of Fire

So I've forgotten nothing, but if I had,
I would still remember this: one evening after
working late to finish out a load of drill pipe
when Maria drove up as usual to take us home
but made us wait in the car with the headlights on.

So we waited, high beams bright as stage lights against
the big front door in the midnight dark. We heard
the electric lift begin to hum as the door rose
slowly to reveal, inside, Maria in her white slip.
No music. Just wind pushing bunchgrass against
a stack of cold roll and the rattle of a strip
of tin siding somewhere. And she began to dance.
Against a backdrop of iron and steel, looming hulks
of lathes and drill presses, tools scattered in the grease
and dirt, this still lithe, slim, small-boned creature
began to move silently, just the dry, eggshell
shuffle of her feet against the floor, began to glide,
leaping, spinning, rising, settling like a paper
tossed and floating in a breeze. I saw her then the way
young men must have seen Isadora Duncan once,
the first time. And I remember thinking, so this
is how it was, had been, for her on stage in Paris
or California when there was a future in her life.
The idling engine made the headlights shudder
so her body shimmered in a kind of silver foam,
and then turning quickly in a sweeping motion
into the center of the light, she stopped, froze,
head lifted in profile, wide-eyed, looking astonished
and a little fearful, a face that I had seen before,
and late that night I found it in my Gombrich's:
the orphan girl, by Delacroix. And I can tell you

that since that evening it's the face I've looked for
in every woman that I've known.

The Journal: *The holy disease without the holiness. Worse, without the*
words. Ex-poet. The X poet. I swallowed my tongue years ago. Bad joke.
But I still pray—a bird, rising. Cendrars: "Mental prayer is the aviary
of God."

                              It all came apart
in L.A., she said, studying me through a wineglass
after Roy had gone to bed. *Roy fell in*
somehow with Robert Rossen, the master craftsman
of screenplays, first writer on Sierra Madre
before Huston took it over. But Rossen was
an ex-Red who at first refused to testify and then
used fronts and pseudonyms, the way they all did
those awful years the blacklist was in force.
They had collaborated on a script about
the Owens River deal: buying up the land
of unsuspecting farmers, posing as agents
of the reclamation project, then rigging up
a bond issue that would bring the water
not to L.A., as advertised, but to land purchased
by the city fathers downtown who thereby
made a ton, believe me. Biggest land scam
in this country's history since Manhattan island.

And no one complained because they all got fat
somewhere down the line as the water poured in
and land values soared. As Roy always said,
it's history's greatest lesson: if enough people
commit a crime, it's not a crime anymore.
And because Roy was not a Red, they put his name
on the manuscript. What a stupid thing to do.
Of course, the script found its way downtown, some strings
were pulled, pressure brought to bear, and suddenly
Roy had no career, especially since through the tie
with Rossen he was suspect anyway. Her voice
was frayed, tough, the wineglass empty, the ashtray full.
So the drinking started, then later, after Bakersfield,
the seizures, more drink, Tegretol, phenobarbital,
Dilantin, the whole mess. But that was years ago.
She made a kind of smile that wavered at the end.
Life's been simplified for us. It's simple now.
But of course she was talking to herself, not me.
And I was thinking, this is it, how lives go on,
this is how it happens, what I do not understand.

But then, this, too, this, too: when I drove her home
one night in early summer and we sat outside
with the pulse of cicadas washing over us in waves.
No talk. But I felt there was something between us.
Her profile blurred by a patchwork of shadows, eyes

stealing the light from the trailer's window. A woman
twenty years my senior. It wasn't sex. Not quite.
God knows, I ached to know a woman, wanted it
so bad I could have cried. In fact, I did. But this was,
well, not even love, more like wonderment. Erotic,
yes, but still, frozen, not to be acted on. She turned
to me *and knew what I knew* and smiled and went in,
or started to, then turned around, walked slowly back,
slid into the seat and still smiling looked at me
a long time before reaching over to place her hand
behind my head and carefully, delicately, as if
there were only a slight coolness moving there,
running the tip of her tongue along my lips.
Until it ended, the earth was breathing, it seemed,
or the space around us had become some sort
of immense beating heart, and when she peeled back
my shirt, and her lips—damp and unmercifully
soft—moved down my chest and belly, I believe
that I was actually trembling, a small wing beating
in my throat as she took me into her mouth
and afterward placed her hand flat on my chest, just so,
as if to say, *a gift, just this once, never again.*

But this was before the summer dust and heat
came down the way it does in July heavy as sleep
so I felt half-drunk running the pipe rack, unloading

flat-bed haulers rumbling in each day, drivers sitting
on their fat asses letting me do all the work, and so
I mashed my foot between two drill collars and spent
the next few days in bed terribly happy reading
Flannery O'Connor and laughing myself well again.
Two or three weeks later, my father called me over.
Take a look. At his feet lay a sort of concrete bullet,
or bomb, sand-colored, with what seemed little flecks
of glass on the tapered part. *You know what that is?*
Well, that's the end of the story, bud. His foot nudged
the nose of the thing as if it were a dead deer.
The diamond bit. Chunks of low-grade diamond embedded
in the cutting surface. Can drill through anything.
So the old tri-cone's out. With this one they can stay
in the hole forever, and you know what that means.
And I did. Almost our whole business was threading pipe.
On oil rigs, pulling five thousand feet of drill pipe
in and out of the hole to change bits damaged
pipe joints. With the new bit, less damage, less work.
For us, a lot less. Not enough to make a profit.
Not even enough to pay costs. Amazing. And so,
it was all over, or soon would be. I looked at the face
of my father staring into the future, at the shop
he had built, the lathes lined up along the north side,
their iron song almost unbroken through twenty years,
the never-washed, grease-laden windows, gutted drawworks,

gears, bushings, tools spilled across the now scarred,
cement floor where I had worked every summer
since I was ten. And then a feather grazed my ear,
the ruffle of wings, and a vision rose in my head:
I was free. My future lay clear and open and bright
as the treeless field across the road. The burden
of inheritance now lifted, vanished. No shop.
Anything: musician, writer, anything I wanted.
I walked out into an endless sky. I rose. I flew.

The death of the shop was slow. Over the next year
or so work tapered off, as we knew it would,
and the welders and machinists walked away,
slowly, one by one. My father found other jobs
for them, in Midland, Snyder, towns like that,
and I put off college for a year to pick up the slack.
Roy and Maria dropped by the house on their way
out of town, Buick idling in the driveway, top down.
Come here, she said. She kissed my forehead, *Be good
to the girls, treat them right*. And Roy lit a cigar
and pointed to a box of books beside the car:
Read, learn a thing or two. They could have been going
to a wedding, all eager and bright, *nothing wrong here,*
and the car swaggered out, crunching gravel and squealing
onto Highway 54 with that Airstream trailer

gleaming in the distance, a silver sun floating
on heat waves along a straight black line of asphalt
to Route 66 and whatever would happen next.

Roy died a year later of a brain aneurism
at Maria's sister's house while he was watching
a Dodgers game on TV. He always said
that when the Dodgers moved from Brooklyn to L.A.,
the world began to die. Well, I guess it did.
I came home from college for Christmas break
to find the Buick in our driveway. *Maria had it
driven here,* my father said. *After Roy died,
she didn't want it. She wanted you to have it.*
When he handed me the title, placed in my palm
that small, pink slip of paper with Maria's name
on it, it lay in my hand until my hand moved,
which was a long time.

                    Along with it was a message
about the Buick's trunk, where I found a box
marked ROY'S STUFF, and inside Maria's note:

*It's not much, most of it from the Paris years, tip of the iceberg, really,
a lot written but a ton thrown away. After L.A., Roy could never finish
anything. I think he never wanted to see it take final form. Always
possible, but not quite there. You could say he fell in love with the blank*

page, the about-to-be-written. You know his rules: pay attention,
forget nothing, worship the imagination. And he followed them, even
if there's not much left to show.

And then she gave her sister's address in L.A.
I looked the poems over, a mystery to me then,
though I've begun to see now, I believe, the ghosts
of Cendrars, Ponge, and Char standing over them.
And at the bottom of the box were pages photocopied
from a journal with this entry among the others:

It goes on. It goes on and on. Tonight, after dinner. We danced.
The old music. We have nothing, really. Nothing but ourselves.

That something may remain. When I returned from college
that next summer, the trucking business was picking up,
and my father and I began to think that we could turn
the shop to making custom truck beds. Make some money.
Stay afloat. Besides, college was such a disappointment.
Nobody read there. Well, maybe the professors,
in their "area of specialty," if that means anything.
Who could have known? There was a farm kid from Sublette
who said he came to learn Italian to read Dante
the way he should be read, but he transferred out.
I could write better, anyway, at home, I thought.
I was pretty lonely. But there were still the movies,

where I spent my extra time. When I drove there
one Friday night that winter, it had snowed, heavy,
about five inches, and I hadn't even bothered
to brush it off the car. The movie wasn't much,
but there was one scene I can't forget. A man,
a lonely small-town jeweler who is deaf and mute,
has that day lost his best friend, the friend he loves,
and as he walks the streets blind with grief, his hands
begin to move across his chest in sign language.
He is talking to himself. His hands move swiftly,
furiously, like small birds fighting in midair, then
faster, a blur, the mad flight of a man's hands
speaking hugely but silently, clamoring,
crying out, . . . and then it stops. The hands drop
to his sides. Without motion. Without speech.
A man walks down the street with his hands at his sides,
and so does everyone else. And who can tell
the difference?
                        Strange to think of all this now—
another time, another country, where I look down
each night on the lights of Paris littering the river—
but when I emerged from darkness into the coarse glare
of street lamps, it had warmed up, and walking toward
the car, I could see the snow melting and dropping off,
small pieces sliding off the hood and down the fenders,
the big Buick rising from the snow with patches

of watery blue emerging as it rose. I stopped
ten feet or so away and stared at it, astonished,
stunned, *that coming into being still going on,*
as the white top snow-laden beneath the street lamp
gave off rainbow colors, iridescent, the hard fire
of a thousand jewels, and wherever on the metal
the snow had melted was the glazed blue, looking
brilliant, deeper, bluer than it had ever been.
I stood there a long time listening to the soft crush
of clumps of snow as they dropped onto the street and then,
in the background, hearing the night sounds of horns
far away and a lone shout somewhere close by
and watching the lights in the gleaming blue surface
from passing cars and from the stars and the moon
and from anywhere there was any light at all
as all things seen and unseen and all kingdoms
naked in the human heart rose toward the sky.

Mlle Pym

from *Three Poems by Roy Eldridge Garcia*

On Saturday Mlle Pym would marry a philatelist, and her relatives had decided to boycott the wedding. They were as tolerant as the next person, but since the death of Uncle Max, an assistant postmaster, stamps had been banished from the family. Uncle Max was a funny man, full of laughter and clever banter, and even a single stamp resting in one's palm seemed cruelly to point to his absence, his wit that had brightened the house for some fifty years. However, Mlle Pym, who loathed Uncle Max's stale jokes, felt no qualms about yielding to the philatelist's advances, awkward as they were. The announcement of their wedding was sent by special delivery. Each wedding invitation carried ten five-centime stamps, each of a different color. So when the couple found only strangers at the wedding, they were angered but not surprised. The ceremony was flawless, and emerging from the church, the bride and her philatelist were showered with stamps from all countries, of every hue and shape. There was Portugal, green with rose edging, and quaint Bolivia, imperial in its bold blue. And fluttering ominously down to rest in the bride's outstretched hand was Iceland, pale and triangular, damp from the tongue of a stranger.

The Deposition

Dust storm, we thought, a brown swarm
plugging the lungs, or a locust cloud,
but this was a collapse, a slow sinking
to deeper brown, and deeper still, like the sky
seen from inside a well as we are lowered down,
and the air twisting and tearing at itself.

But it was done. And the body hung there
like a butchered thing, naked and alone
in a sudden hush among the ravaged air.
The ankles first—slender, blood-caked,
pale in the sullen dark, legs broken
below the knees, blue bruises smoldering
to black. And the spikes. We tugged iron
from human flesh that dangled like limbs
not fully hacked from trees, nudged
the cross beam from side to side until
the sign that mocked him broke loose.
It took all three of us. We shouldered the body
to the ground, yanked nails from wrists
more delicate, it seemed, than a young girl's
but now swollen, gnarled, black as burnt twigs.
The body, so heavy for such a small man,
was a knot of muscle, a batch of cuts

and scratches from the scourging, and down
the right side a clotted line of blood,
the sour posca clogging his ragged beard,
the eyes exploded to a stare that shot
through all of us and still speaks in my dreams:
I know who you are.
     So, we began to wash
the body, wrenching the arms, now stiff
and twisted, to his sides, unbending
the ruined legs and sponging off the dirt
of the city, sweat, urine, shit—all the body
gives—from the body, laying it out straight
on a sheet of linen rank with perfumes
so that we could cradle it, haul it
to the tomb. The wind shouted.
The foul air thickened. I reached over
to close the eyes. *I know who you are.*

A Starlit Night

All over America at this hour men are standing
by an open closet door, slacks slung over one arm,
staring at wire hangers, thinking of taxes
or a broken faucet or their first sex: the smell
of back-seat Naugahyde, the hush of a maize field
like breathing, the stars rushing, rushing away.

And a woman lies in an unmade bed watching
the man she has known twenty-one, no,
could it be? twenty-two years, and she is listening
to the polonaise climbing up through radio static
from the kitchen where dishes are piled
and the linoleum floor is a great, gray sea.

It's the A-flat polonaise she practiced endlessly,
never quite getting it right, though her father,
calling from the darkened TV room, always said,
"Beautiful, kiddo!" and the moon would slide across
the lacquered piano top as if it were something
that lived underwater, something from far below.

They both came from houses with photographs,
the smell of camphor in closets, board games
with missing pieces, sunburst clocks in the kitchen

that made them, each morning, a little sad.
They didn't know what they wanted, every night,
every starlit night of their lives, and now they have it.

Motion Sickness

I am tired of the heave and swell,
the deep lunge in the belly, the gut's
dumb show of dance and counterdance,
sway and pause, the pure jig of nausea
in the pit of a spinning world.
Where the body moves, the mind
often lags, clutching deck, anchor,
the gray strap that hangs like the beard
of death from the train's ceiling,
the mind lost in the slow bulge
of ocean under the moon's long pull
or the endless coil of some medieval
argument for the existence of God
or the dream of the giant maze
that turns constantly in and in
on itself and there is no way out . . .
I am sick and tired of every rise and fall
of the sun, the moon's tedious cycle
that sucks blood from the thighs of women
and turns teenage boys into wolves
prowling the streets, hungry for motion.
Let me be still, let me rest
in some hollow of space and time
far from the seasons and that boring,
ponderous drama of day and night.
Let me sleep in the heart of calm

and dream placidly of birds frozen
in the unmoving air of eternity
and the earth grown immobile
in its centrifugal spin, and God
motionless as Lazarus in his tomb
before he is raised dizzily
to fall again, to rise, to fall.

A Wall Map of Paris

. . . tragend als Strömung das Haupt und die Leier.
    —RILKE

A night of drinking, dawn is coming on,
my friend's hand falls along a darkening stain
that runs from Vaugirard to Palatine
and west to rue Cassette. *There,* he says,
*Rilke wrote "The Panther." And that darkness
came from James Wright's head one soggy night
when he drank too much, leaned back into the Seine,
and recited verse till dawn.* Ohio sunlight
stuns the windowpane, and I'm seeing Paris,
where the morning bronzes cobblestones,
the grates around the chestnut trees, and a man
with a fullback's shoulders and a dancer's tread
whistles a Schubert tune and walks toward
a river like the rivers in his head.

He looks for Villon's ghost at Notre Dame,
recalls Apollinaire, the rain-soaked heart
of sad Verlaine, Rilke at the Dome,
and later at St. Anne's watches children
learning how to *faire la bise.* But on
Pont Neuf, when he gazes deep into the Seine,
the face of a glassworker's son stares back,
and the river that runs through Paris runs
through Ohio past Jimmy Leonard's shack,
the Shreve High Football Stadium, and Kenyon,

where a boy with the memory of a god
and a gift for taking images to heart
translates from a poem about the head
of Orpheus, in a river, singing.

At the Café de Flore

This evening as I am entering the Café de Flore to buy some cigarettes, I meet Levastine with a half-drunken companion who introduced himself as the "abbé défroqué surréaliste." He was the first surrealist priest.

—MIRCEA ELIADE, *JOURNAL I, 1945–1955*

I have anointed boutonnieres and cats,
preached homilies on spectacles and bats,
baptized the morning, evening, and full moon,
and blessed both happiness and gloom.
I proclaim the doctrine of broken clocks:
on every hour, remove your shoes and socks,
sing the Marseillaise nine times backwards
and consider, please, the lives of birds
(there are fewer than before the war).
Père Surréaliste does not wish to bore
with his prayers to orchids and champagne,
the sanctity of wine, the uselessness of pain,
but thirty miles from here are flowers
growing from the mouths of boys.
For what I've seen there is no word,
I am the Priest of the Absurd.

At Omaha Beach

Lewis M. Ginsberg
d. June 7, 1944

The waves wash out, wash in.
The rain comes down. It comes down.
The sky runs into the sea
that turns in its troubled sleep,
dreaming its long gray dream.
White stars stand on the lawn.
We move on the edges of speech.

Sleep comes down. It comes down.
Dreams wash out, wash in.
Our fathers walk out of the sea.
The air is heavy with speech.
Our fathers are younger than we.
As the fog dissolves in the dawn,
our fathers lie down on the beach.

We're a dream drifting down on a beach
in the rain in the sleep of our lives.
White stars wash over a lawn.
We are troubled by sea and sky.
Our words dissolve in the waves.
On the edges of speech is the sound
of the rain coming down. It comes down.

The Memory Palace

The next stage is memory, which is like a great field or a
spacious palace. . . . It is a vast, immeasurable sanctuary.
Who can plumb its depths? And yet it is a faculty of my soul.
Although it is part of my nature, I cannot understand all that I
am. This means, then, that the mind is too narrow to contain
itself entirely. But where is that part of it which it does not itself
contain? Is it somewhere outside itself and not within it? How,
then, can it be a part of it, if it is not contained in it?

—ST. AUGUSTINE, *CONFESSIONS*

He inferred that persons desiring to train this faculty (of
memory) must select places and form mental images of the
things they wish to remember and store those images in the
places, so that the order of the places will preserve the order of
things, and the images of the things will denote the things
themselves, . . .

—CICERO IN *DE ORATORE*,
SPEAKING OF THE POET SIMONIDES

. . . and he taught me Bruno's memory system, the nearest thing
to immortality, he said, for then I would forget nothing, and
everything would be imprinted on my soul.

—"THE BLUE BUICK"

It is dark but will soon be light. We will place them here, in each
room, on each machine, each part your hands touched repeatedly,
all those surfaces glossed now with moonlight raining through the
slats in the roof.

There is a certain urgency about this, like the undertow at Galveston
when you almost drowned. A certain pull.

It is the machine shop, of course, because you saw your father build it and your mother worry over it and both of them quarrel and grieve over it, and you worked there, and it became the air your family breathed, the food they ate. It is all around you and inside you, and for reasons you cannot know, it contains everything you did or felt or thought.

There is, first, your version of paradise, Avenue J in Houston, your father just back from the war, a working-class neighborhood before television pulled everyone inside, all the fathers home from work, mothers calling from front porches, and all your people—Bert, Locie, your sister, Marie, your aunt and uncle—sitting on blankets in the backyard, the good talk and laughter as night comes on, and to commemorate this, along with the things of your life, we place throughout the shop, draped across the backs of lathes and drill presses and milling machines, the sentences you never want to forget, sentences from the first prose you ever read that made the word *beauty* form in your mind and made you want to write, to write sentences.

> *On the rough wet grass of the back yard my father and mother have spread quilts. We all lie there, my mother, my father, my uncle, my aunt, and I too am lying there.*

Out back in the welding shop where men were gods, Vulcans in black helmets, and the blaze of cutting torches hurled onto the ceiling the gigantic shadows you watched as a child, place here the things of gods and children: baseball; a twilight doubleheader and the blue bowl of the sky as the lights came on; the fragrance of mown grass in the outfield; the story about the great pitcher, Moses Yellowhorse; your first double play at second base, the feeling of having your body disappear inside a motion; O.T. Swearingen holding his infant grandson in the shadow of the door of the great barn where it was always night; the storm cellar; the great yawn of the door, and then the going down, the rank earth smells, the swallowing up.

In the center, next to the grinder, place the image of your grandmother, her legs ribbed with varicose veins. O.T., haunted by night terrors, would call out in his sleep, *Nellie, Nellie.* In the morning in the kitchen with the slanted floor, you would stare at her legs, the purple cords, and think, she has walked so far in this kitchen, has walked to another country, and O.T. was calling her back.

> *First we were sitting up, then one of us lay down, and then we all lay down, on our stomachs, or on our sides, or on our backs, and they have kept on talking.*

In the tool-and-die shed that has no windows, things seen in half-light, dimly remembered and almost—but not quite—understood: the woman who scavenged trash cans late at night wearing a high school formal, walking the alleys, the tin clutter of her life rattling through the town; standing in line at the supermarket yesterday, there it was in your head, the hum of the lathe, song of the honing cloth, a child's song heard from a distance; shooting hoops after sunset, the whisper of the net in the darkness, the surrounding silence.

They are not talking much, and the talk is quiet, of nothing in particular, of nothing at all in particular, of nothing at all.

The fireworks display at the softball field. Early evening, chorus of cicadas behind you. The eyes of your children sparkling with reflected light. You have no words for bliss and so lose yourself in the stars. On the way home, everyone sings "If You've Got the Money, I've Got the Time." Drape this over the lathe your father worked, days and sometimes nights, for twenty-seven years.

The stars are wide and alive, they seem each like a smile of great sweetness, and they seem very near.

Over here, in the lap of the big drill press, where the drill froze and you panicked, place all things sudden: Uncle Harry breaking into a Fred Astaire soft-shoe; waking in Kansas to snowfall—the hush, the heart's cathedral, the last echoes of the choir floating down, your breath fogging the window, bleaching the trees; the great dust storm, crawling home on your hands and knees so you could feel the sidewalk; old Mrs. Pate's elm clogged with grackles, then bursting in a chattering black cloud of feathers and falling leaves.

All my people are larger bodies than mine, quiet, with voices gentle and meaningless like the voices of sleeping birds.

The field on the west is dressed out with tropes; Keats's untrodden region of the mind, Dickinson's cathedral tunes, Donne's compass, Jarrell's "waist the spirit breaks its arm on," all the ones in Plath's "Medallion." Nearest, just opposite the big pipe straightener, will be the first ones, from the Old Testament, invisible to fundamentalists. And you will always need them because you hunger always for things seen in the light of everything else, and the light is endless.

The strangest event in your life, your baptism, because you walked through a doorway but arrived in the same room: place it here, in the office where the elderly bookkeeper, Mr. Mayfield, kept meticulous records. An inventory. And your mother weeping because your life was saved, rescued, like Jimmy Deeds pulled from the river, still breathing. Saved, accounted for.

One is my mother who is good to me. One is my father who is good to me.

On the faceplate of the milling machine, where iron fillings spilled into a child's outstretched hands, place things felt, the biography of your skin: falling off to sleep, the cool palms of the sheets, the lightness of your body; your first French kiss, your hand on the small breasts of Samantha Dobbins, her belly, her thigh, the astonishing softness, her quickening breath in the shallow of your neck; waves lapping your ankles like little mouths; the pugil stick in your stomach, a voice saying, *You have been here before;* the nail in the foot; the car wreck when you were four, touching your mother's face, the tiny slivers of glass flickering red and blue in the police car's lights.

On the top shelf of this iron cabinet, circling the toolbox, the ornaments of labor: the time card, punched, with eight hours remaining; *The Machinist's Handbook;* the metal hard hat with the leather lining smelling of thirty years of sweat; the aluminum black lunch box with the Captain Marvel decal, the copy of Fitzgerald's *Odyssey* inside; the steel burr they removed from your father's eye, work gloves lying in the gathering bin, where he threw them.

By some chance, here they are, all on this earth . . . lying, on quilts, on the grass, in a summer evening, among the sounds of the night.

And this, on the iron beam where the sparrows gathered: St. Joseph's Hospital, and through the big window you watched two large birds in the distance, two white flames swooping in great, crossing arcs against the leaves of date palms, and you concentrated hard on that until the pain in your lungs fell away, diminished until it seemed very distant, hardly there at all. You were astonished at the beauty, the mystery, of the birds. One, you decided, was Time. The other, Being.

After a little, I am taken in and put to bed.

And this: in the backyard of the little white rent-house with the Spanish moss hanging down, tossing a Frizbee to your son, and when his small body curved up and out to catch it, a beam of light broke over the corner of the house and passed between his fingertips and the orange disk, and time froze, and three hundred years later he came down and you rose to get another beer from the refrigerator.

All of this, and more, you must hang onto, you must, but time is running out, here is your daughter on stage, a goddess, the beauty of it is overwhelming; your son rounding the bases the first time, grinning; your wife, oh this one, with her face veiled in shadows, the eyes weary, a life written across her forehead, her hand touching your wrist, that touch, that evening.

Sleep, soft smiling, draws me unto her: and those receive me, who quietly treat me, as one familiar and well-beloved in that home: but will not, oh, will not, not now, not ever; but will not ever tell me who I am.

Along the bedways of the small lathe, where the long window gathered the afternoon light and you could feel the last layers of the workday falling away, place these: an orange grove in California, 1944, the songlike, soprano voices of women lifting and falling; your first library book, *Biography of a Grizzly,* read on the corner of 3rd and Kansas, the traffic of the world suddenly frozen around you; the high school photo of Patricia Lea Gillespie, a little frightened, the future coming on too fast, too fast; a small boy in a T-shirt that says, I'D RATHER BE IN PHILADELPHIA; a girl with her hair in a bun, dancing for her aunts and uncles, who have promised to cover their eyes; your old friend Radke's painting, *The Arrival of the Future,* the future a halo of wasps around his head; your uncle Bill Branum, the funniest man you ever knew, dying of lung cancer, hand dropping onto a steel tray, cigarette ash floating across a white tile floor; the beach at Galveston at sunset, lavender glass and chrome of the waves flattening out, the last light dragged out to sea, darkening sand, voices of your kinfolk lifting gull-like, that flight of laughter, twilight glimmer of beer cans, a black dog, cigarettes, faces squinting at the sun; the sun.

May god bless my people, my uncle, my aunt, my mother, my good father, oh, remember them kindly in their time of trouble; and in the hour of their taking away.

And this: the day during a viral fever you felt your Self detaching itself and moving like a boat unmoored from a dock slowly but irretrievably away from your body, and the terror was more real than your body. Do not forget this, for it was hell. Hang this from the hook of the center hoist.

Look around, see how they are all positioned, each in its place. Now you can remember everything. But there's no more time, it's morning, time to go to work, and they are opening the huge shop door, that slow rumble you will never forget, and the light leaking in, widening—light like a quilt of gold foil flung out so it will drape all of this, will keep it and keep it well—and it is so bright now, you can hardly bear it as it fills the door, this immense glacier of light coming on, and still you do not know who you are, but here it is, try to remember, it is all beginning:

Usher

(2009)

The Gray Man

We are cutting weeds and sunflowers on the shoulder,
the gray man and I, red dust coiling up around us,
muddying our sweat-smeared mugs, clogging our hair,
the iron heel of an August Kansas sun pushing down
on the scythes we raise against it and swing down
in an almost homicidal rage and drunken weariness.
And I keep my distance. He's a new hire just off
the highway, a hitchhiker sick to death of hunger,
the cruelties of the road, and our boss hates
poverty just enough to hire it, even this old man,
a dead, leaden pall upon his skin so vile it makes you
pull away, the gray trousers and state-issue black
prison boots, the bloodless, grim, unmoving lips,
and the eyes set in concrete, dark hallways that lead
to darker rooms down somewhere in the basement
of the soul's despair. Two weeks. He hasn't said
a word. *He's a goddamned ghost,* I tell my father.
Light flashes from his scythe as he decapitates
big clumps of yellow blooms, a flailing, brutal war
against the lords of labor, I suppose, against the state,
the world, himself, who knows. When we break,
I watch the canteen's water bleed from the corners
of his mouth, a spreading wound across his shirt,
the way he spits into the swollen pile of bluestem
and rank bindweed as if he hates it and everything
that grows, a hatred that has roots and thickens,

twisting, snarled around itself. A lizard wanders
into sunlight, and he hacks at it, chopping clods
until dust clouds rise like mist around him, and then
he speaks in a kind of shattering of glass cutting
through the hot wind's sigh, the fear: *Love thine enemy.*
He says it to the weeds or maybe what they stand for.
Then, knees buckling, with a rasping, gutted sob
as if drowning in that slough of dirty air, he begins,
trembling, to cry.

              I was a boy. The plains' wind
leaned against the uncut weeds. High wires hummed
with human voices in their travail. And the highway
I had worked but never traveled lay across the fields
and vanished in that distant gray where day meets night.

Trilogy

Truly, thou art a God who hidest thyself.

—ISAIAH 45:15

I think of cinemas, panoramic sleights
With multitudes bent toward some flashing scene
Never disclosed, but hastened to again,
Foretold to other eyes on the same screen . . .
  —HART CRANE, "TO BROOKLYN BRIDGE"

The "meters," *chandas*, are the robes that the gods "wrapped around themselves," *acchadayan*, so that they might come near to the fire without being disfigured as though by the blade of a razor.

  —ROBERT CALASSO, *LITERATURE AND THE GODS,*
    COMMENTING ON THE *SATAPUTHA BRAHMANA*

Frieda Pushnik

"Little Frieda Pushnik, the Armless, Legless Girl
Wonder," who spent years as a touring attraction for
Ripley's Believe It or Not and Ringling Brothers and
Barnum and Bailey . . .

—"OBITUARIES," *LOS ANGELES TIMES*

These are the faces I love. Adrift with wonder,
big-eyed as infants and famished for that *strangeness*
in the world they haven't known since early childhood.
They are monsters of innocence who gladly shoulder
the burden of the blessed, the unbroken, the beautiful,
the lost. They should be walking on their lovely knees
like pilgrims to that shrine in Guadalupe, where
I failed to draw a crowd. I might even be their weird
little saint, though God knows *I've wanted everything
they've wanted,* and more, of course. When we toured Texas,
west from San Antonio, those tiny cow towns flung
like pearls from the broken necklace of the Rio Grande,
I looked out on a near-infinity of rangeland
and far blue mountains, avatars of emptiness,
minor gods of that vast and impossibly pure nothing
to whom I spoke my little stillborn, ritual prayer.

I'm not on those posters they paste all over town,
those silent orgies of secondary colors—jade,
burnt orange, purple—each one a shrieking anthem
to the exotic: Bengal tigers, ubiquitous
as alley cats, raw with not inhuman but
superhuman beauty, demonic spider monkeys,

absurdly buxom dancers clad in gossamer,
and spiritual gray elephants, trunks raised like arms
to Allah. Franciscan murals of plenitude,
brute vitality ripe with the fruit of eros,
the faint blush of sin, and I am not there. Rather,
my role is the unadvertised, secret, wholly
unexpected thrill you find within. A discovery.
Irresistible, like sex.

     So here I am. The crowd
leaks in—halting, unsure, a bit like mourners
at a funeral but without the grief. And there is
always something damp, interior, and, well,
sticky about them, cotton-candy souls that smear
the bad air, funky, bleak. All, quite forgettable,
except for three. A woman, middle-aged, plain
and unwrinkled as her Salvation Army uniform,
bland as oatmeal but with this heavy, leaden sorrow
pulling at her eyelids and the corners of her mouth.
Front row four times, weeping, weeping constantly,
then looking up, lips moving in a silent prayer,
I think, and blotting tears with a kind of practiced,
automatic movement somehow suggesting that
the sorrow is her own and I'm her mirror now,
the little well of suffering from which she drinks.
A minister once told me to embrace my sorrow.
To hell with that, I said, *embrace your own.* And then

there was that nice young woman, Arbus, who came and talked,
talked brilliantly, took hours setting up the shot,
then said, *I'm very sorry,* and just walked away.
The way the sunlight plunges through the opening
at the top around the center tent pole like a spotlight
cutting through the smutty air, and it fell on him,
the third, a boy of maybe sixteen, hardly grown,
sitting in the fourth row, not too far but not too close,
red hair flaring numinous, ears big as hands,
gray eyes that nailed themselves to mine. My mother,
I remember, looked at me that way. And a smile
not quite a smile. He came twice. And that second time,
just before I thanked the crowd, *I'm so glad you could
drop by, please tell your friends,* his hand rose—floated,
really—to his chest. It was a wave. The slightest,
shyest wave good-bye, hello (and what's the difference,
anyway) as if he knew me, *truly* knew me, as if,
someday, he might return. His eyes. His hair, as vivid
as the howdahs on those elephants. In the posters
where I'm not. That day the crowd seemed to slither out,
to ooze, I thought, like reptiles—sluggish, sleek, gut-hungry
for the pleasures of the world, the prize, the magic number,
the winning shot, the doll from the rifle booth, the girl
he gives it to, the snow cone dripping, the popcorn dyed
with all the colors of the rainbow, the *rainbow,* the sky
it crowns, and whatever lies beyond, the One, perhaps,

we're told, enthroned there who in love or rage or spasm
of inscrutable desire made that teeming, oozing,
devouring throng borne now into the midway's sunlight,
that vanished, forever silent God to whom I say
again my little prayer: *let me be one of them.*

Usher

1954, Nathan Gold, a student at Union Theological Seminary, working part-time at the Loews 83rd Street Theater, Manhattan

Dear Sollie,
              Master of Kaballah, each cryptic point
of David's star, now casting I Ching hexagrams
in hipster Berkeley. So this one's in hexameters,
an undercurrent, roughly six feet under—no,
not death, but bad news, fear and failure, everywhere:
Robert Moses, goddamned Cross Bronx Expressway,
the parting of the Red Sea is what that fascist bastard
thinks, I'm betting, though the Golds were never Reds
except for Uncle Mike, and now where do they go,
exiled from their homeland and beloved Yankees.
And Sivan in her condition. And their turncoat son
leading goyim and Manhattan's great unwashed
down dark aisles to pray before the gleaming gods
of Hollywood, returning each day to the classrooms
of German theologians for whom God is a puzzle,
a conundrum made darker yet by that Danish Rabbi,
Kierkegaard. So here I wait, lean on gilded,
faux-Moroccan walls, and stare worshipfully
at plaster masks of tragedy and big-mouthed
comedy hung overhead, blue-green bulbs
for eyes that blindly gaze not at but over us,
lost in their abstractions and detached as always
from the laity, their stench and squalor, floors pocked
with Dubble Bubble and the stale, mingled smells

of soda, buttered popcorn, licorice, and ammonia.
Mr. Hinkle, our gin-head manager, has passed out
in the upstairs office once again, and Brownie,
the homunculus projectionist, is no doubt reading
fuck books and sucking Jujubes and Milk Duds
while I wait, armed with flashlight and Kierkegaard,
that monster, *Either/Or,* because my paper's overdue
(though useless, really, after yesterday's debacle).
Are those made happy by *A Star Is Born,* warmed
by love's ruin and resurrection in *The Country Girl*
really in *despair?* Churchyard, that joy killer,
thinks so. I say, let them wallow in the shallows
of the silver screen, the smart-assed repartee of Tracy
and brainy Hepburn, the lurid Technicolor charms
of Vista Vision, Gene Kelly dancing in the rain,
Gary Cooper's quick-draw Jesus in *High Noon.*
Tillich just won't stop with his *ultimate concern,*
ground of being, courage of despair, his *God*
above God, and in between, *illusions*: movies, yes,
but more, the life that copies them. Crossing Eighth,
I saw a woman, hair swept across one eye
like Rita Hayworth, walk into a bus-stop bench.
Blind humanity. Niebuhr would have loved it,
Tillich, too, *the grandeur and the misery,* New York,
the world, everything's a metaphor to them.
But misery like Sivan's, glioblastoma multiforme,

do they know *that,* those Graeco-Latin syllables
baroque and swollen as the thing itself, fat tumor
feeding on the brain, burning from the center
out, and those prick doctors without the balls to give
one cc more Dilaudid than the law allows.
So there I am, just another addict trafficking
in horse among the freaks of Hubert's Dime Museum
and scoring D from the trembling future surgeon
who uses it to pay tuition. God, the crap
we do to make a life. *Sin?* The *world* is sin.
We go down, oh, I mean *down,* into that basement:
Jesus, those little stages dim with burnt-out bulbs,
the curtains jerk back, lo, and there is lovely Olga
and her beard, Sealo the Seal Boy, The Armless Wonder,
Albert-Alberta in his/her hermaphroditic glory.
Baudelaire's "floating lives," or as Sivan said,
"Disneyland in hell." But, of course, they're us,
we're them, and we pay the price, cheap as it is, to see
ourselves.
          Ah, New York when she was well: Al Flosso's
magic shop on 34th, my God, late Saturday
one afternoon strolling down from Central Park,
bronze leaves spilled like coins along Eighth Avenue,
and there's Al himself pulling quarters from the ears
of little kids who spend them all on props, Zombies,
Imp Bottles, Crazy Cubes, tricks for turning water

into wine, if happiness is wine made holy,
and I think it is, or was. Later, fine dining
at the Automat to save a buck, Eucharist
at Smokey Mary's, then all those jazz clubs lining
52nd Street, and that's the night at Birdland
the great Eddie "Lockjaw" Davis went toe-to-toe
with Sonny Stitt. *Pure heaven.* Jimmy Ryan's, Five Spot,
The Famous Door, Three Deuces, Sivan's long auburn
hair now gone but brilliant then, bathed in neon,
big riffs streaming out of every door, a kind
of aural exegesis of forbidden texts:
"Love for Sale," "Strange Fruit," "Ornithology."

Long time passing. Then yesterday in systematics
Tillich demolishing Parmenides by way
of Plato's *Sophist: Any image is a blending:*
Nonbeing closed in Being (my loose translation).
And so the movies, the technology of film:
the image held before our flawed, half-blind gaze,
black ribs separating every frame, that darkness
never seen but always there: in *On the Waterfront,*
Saint and Brando in the fulcrum of their fates,
Manhattan floating in the thinning, pearl-gray light
behind them, and that cinematic night surrounding
every second of their ticking lives, unseen,
ubiquitous: Nonbeing, nothingness, the ontic

absence at the center, or between the frames,
of the waking life. "I could have been a contender
instead of . . . what I am," pleads Brando to his brother:
who he's *not* held forever in the embrace of who he *is*.
"*Persistence of vision,*" I tell Tillich, *that's what it's called,
the fantasy of life in motion while in fact
a little death, NONBEING, separates each frame,
each moment in the shadow play of happiness,
and God in all His wisdom is the projectionist!
THAT'S OUR METAPHOR! Wrong God,* he says. *The God
that can be known cannot be God.* Well, that finished it.
I swear, the man's a neo-Gnostic, a magician.
Imagine, the greatest theologian in America,
a Bronx Jew shouting at him: *THEN WHO THE FUCK
IS GOD?* So, THE END. Alpha and Omega. Sivan
said from the beginning it would end this way.

I'm an usher, Sol. That's all. Light in hand, I take
them down, or up, the Heraclitean way, into
that little night, into—no, not Plato's cave, Lascaux,
or Rheims—but the purest form of K's *aesthetic* life,
and there they sit with the passivity of angels,
God's children in their ontic moment, looking on,
amused, uplifted, frightened, haunted, grieved, lost
in the deceptions of *the beautiful,* the real unreal,
and they are for those ninety stolen minutes *saved*:

Pavlic, from the corner newsstand, shutting down
for matinees—war films, westerns; Mrs. Kriegan,
who cleans bathrooms at St. Bart's and weeps through all
the love scenes; Sivan, too—turbaned, thin—at every
bargain twilight show for *Singin' in the Rain,*
she knew all the tunes and sang them sotto voce
on the subway home; that sad, small man who wore
Hawaiian ties, a Dodgers cap, and tennis shoes,
saying, every time, the rosary on his way out.
All of them, the drunks, bums, lovers, priests, housewives,
cops, street punks shooting up, whores giving blowjobs
in the balcony. I usher. I take them there.

Remember Colmar, the Isenheim, when we were high
on weed, big brass gong of the risen sun, His hands
pushing outward from within, and you, my brother,
in your reefer madness, cactus, and who knows what
shouting "Fire" till I could bring you down? Today
in *Country Girl,* Grace Kelly at the ironing board,
and Brownie upstairs falls asleep at the projector, film
sticking, flap, flap, then stuck, no one to turn the lamp off,
small ghosts of smoke, a black hole starting in the center
of the frame, (the Big Bang must have looked like that),
flame eating outward at the curling edges, spreading,
Grace swallowed slowly by the widening fire, then gone,
the film snaps, bringing down an avalanche of light,

the sun's flood a billion years from now, earth sucked
into the flames, lurid, omnivorous, the whole room
stunned and silvered with it, shadows peeled away,
each gray scarf, each shawl of darkness lifted, the audience
revealed in all their nakedness, their *uncoveredness*
and soiled humanity, among the candy wrappers,
condoms, butts, crushed Dixie cups, as we wait for Grace
to reappear, the iron to move, the mouth to speak,
for love, Sol, the movie of our lives, and for Sivan.

Hart Crane in Havana

April 26, 1932: They breakfasted on board before
making their way into Havana, and after Hart had
pointed out the café where they were to meet, . . . he
slipped down a street in the white, gold, and azure
Cuban capital and for one of the few times in his life
disappeared entirely. He wrote postcards . . .

—CLIVE FISHER, *HART CRANE: A LIFE*

And saw thee dive to kiss that destiny
Like one white meteor, sacrosanct and blent
At last with all that's consummate and free
There, where the first and last gods keep thy tent.

—*THE BRIDGE*

Dear Wilbur,

In Havana, Hotel Ambos Mundos,
Orizaba docked six hours, and I'm drinking
Sazeracs (absinthe and bourbon), sans ami
though recall Ramón Novarro in L.A? Second
only to the Hoover in the cupola Grace
caught me with. No adventures here, home soon
if I can face it—empty-handed, Guggenheim
exhausted. View from absinthe-land: blue and gold
like the Maxfield Parrish prints my father used
to decorate his candy boxes.

As ever, Hart

Dear Sambo,

Je ne suis pas Rimbaud! Though once I was.
Her undinal vast belly moonward bends. Such lines

extinct now. Prescription: iodine followed by
a bottle of Mercurochrome, slashing Siqueiros's
portrait with a razor blade. When Lawrence talks of
"going down to the dark gods," he means sex of course
rather than its sister, death. Remember Hartley's tale
of Albert Ryder, standing just outside his hostess's
window watching Christmas dinner? Thank you so much
for inviting me. A freak, Sam, is what I am. So praise
to you and Otto Kahn,

the uninvited heart

Dear Bill,
        Hotel Ambos Mundos (Both Worlds): Art
and Life? Hemingway, Room 511, just checked out
(of which, art or life?) My third Sazerac, memories
of Minsky's, while legs awaken salads in the brain,
and mine's a Waldorf now, Ouspensky's New Model
where time's a motion on some higher spatial plane
(cinema, still photos moving in a dream of time),
and time's running out, compañero, a broken motion,
Icarus in flight. Love to Susan and bambino,

Hart

Dear Lotte,

  Holed up in a hotel bar, I think
Cleveland Charlotte knows me well as anyone,
and when I wrote to you, "The true idea of God
is the only road to happiness," or something close
to that, please tell me what I meant. One morning,
drunk, Cathedral Santa Prisca, I climbed the tower,
rang the bell-rope that gathers God at dawn, though
no God, no waking pilgrims, just the local Law
and, I confess, a music, triple-tongued, vowels
inside of vowels, a kind of happiness. Love. Hart.

Dear Allen,

  "Le Bateau ivre" is prophetic, so now
why not The Bridge? Sometimes I fear it's just some sort
of spiritual boosterism for empire America.
And then there's Winters with his aesthetique morale:
form, meter as the reins to hold in check the wild horse
of the poem. But damn it, METER IS THE HORSE,
the very heartbeat of the horse, so drop the reins—
OK, I'm drunk, but word is more than word in that
or any poem, Jesus, I stood there, 3 a.m.,
on Roebling's cabled god, its welded, sculpted iron
embrace, staring at Manhattan, tears runneling
my face, the magnitude, the awful holiness
and pride of it, waves beating on the piers below,

Dear Grace,

      <u>borne back ceaselessly into the past</u>,
childhood poems you read to me each night and it
was language, diving down into the language, fall
through consonant and vowel, wash and wave of it,
etymology's dense, green growth, <u>labyrinthine
mouths of history, one arc synoptic of all tides
below</u>. O what lies deepest, meter of the sea,
surge and buffet of what's always underneath
and untranslatable, crucial, crux of everything,
unresurrected Christ, word, in the beginning
now endeth

Key to "Hart Crane in Havana"

I, too, dislike notes—much less a "key"—to poems, but in the case of a realistic imagining of Hart Crane's postcards, written the day before he leaped from the *Orizaba* to his death, such is unavoidable. In his letters it was natural for him, as for anyone writing to friends and relatives, to refer to shared knowledge, names, experiences that would be unknown to most outsiders. Therefore, for those who haven't read Paul Mariani's or Clive Fisher's very fine biographies of Crane, his correspondents as well as some of his allusions need to be identified. All the quoted lines in my poem are from Crane's poems, except for "borne back ceaselessly . . . ," which is taken from the famous final sentence of *The Great Gatsby.*

Wilbur: Wilbur Underwood, poet and government clerk in Washington, DC. He was an older, longtime friend and gay mentor to Crane.

Orizaba: The ship on which Crane and Peggy Cowley were returning to the USA.

Ramón Novarro, Hoover: Fisher reveals in his biography what while living in Pasadena, Crane received the sexual services of the film star, Ramón Novarro, as he had as an adolescent from the Hoover vacuum cleaner his mother, Grace, discovered him with.

Sambo: Sam Loveman, poet and publisher whom Crane met in his early twenties. Loveman was Crane's literary executor and published Brom Weber's *Hart Crane: A Biographical and Critical Study.*

iodine, Mercurochrome, Siqueiros: During his last days in Mexico, Crane made at least two suicide attempts and slashed his portrait by David Siqueiros with a razor blade.

Lawrence: D. H. Lawrence.

Hartley's tale, Albert Ryder: Crane's friend, the artist and poet, Marsden Hartley, tells this story of the painter, Albert Pinkham Ryder. Ryder's hostess asked him why he hadn't come to her Christmas dinner as he had promised, and he explained that he had indeed been there but had been standing outside the window, observing it.

Otto Kahn: Financier who generously underwrote Crane's expenses during the composition of *The Bridge.*

Bill: William Slater Brown. Novelist and translator, he and his wife were old friends of Crane, who had been a guest at their farmhouse in Dutchess County. New York, on several occasions.

Minsky's: The famous Manhattan burlesque theater that Crane and William Slater Brown frequented together and which was probably an influence on Crane's "National Winter Garden."

Ouspensky: Colleague of Gurdjieff and author of *Tertium Organum*, much read and discussed by Crane and his circle.

Lotte: Charlotte Rychtarik, a musician and painter, whom Crane had known since his early twenties in Cleveland.

Allen: Allen Tate, American literary critic and poet and a central member of the Fugitive group of southern poets. He was an early admirer of Crane's work.

"Le Bateau ivre": Rimbaud's famous poem is sometimes interpreted as prophesying the later events of his life.

Winters: Yvor Winters. Prominent literary critic who taught at Stanford University and like Allen Tate was an enthusiastic admirer and advocate of Crane's poetry.

Roebling: Both John Augustus Roebling, architect and builder of the Brooklyn Bridge, and his son, Washington Roebling, who continued his father's work and lived in the same apartment where Crane later wrote *The Bridge*.

Grace: Grace Hart Crane, the poet's mother, divorced from his father in 1917.

The Cottonwood Lounge

It must follow that every infinity is, in a way
we cannot express, made finite to God.

—ST. AUGUSTINE, *DE CIVITATE DEI*

Four boys drinking tomato juice and beer
for God knows why, smoke from Pall Malls
guttering in the floor's red sawdust, the talk
the kind of mindless yak that foams up

when summer is wearing down, and Campbell
is already deep into Cantor and won't shut up,
lining up Coronas to the table's edge
to indicate "infinite progression, just imagine

they go on forever," but Travis, the sad one,
the maniac, who flunked out of A&M playing
bass in pickup bands and chasing girls, just
isn't having it, and says, "But the edge, Campbell,

is there and always will be," and Ira says,
"Please, asshole, just *imagine*," and so it goes,
integers, sets, *transfinite* sets, Coronas filling
the table because "with infinitely small Coronas

this table becomes, my friends, an infinite space
within finite limits," and Travis lip-synching
the Doors' "Break on Through" has carved
IRA CAMPBELL IS A DICK into the soft

lacquered tabletop, and time, illusion though it
may be, argues Ira, is walking past the table
in the form of Samantha Dobbins, all big hair
and legs and brown eyes like storms coming on

who I would date that summer and leave behind
and regret it even now, for time in its linear
progression, real or not, is, I fear, terribly finite,
as it is for God, who, looking down or up

or from some omnidirectional quantum point
in this one universe among many suffers
the idiocies of four beer-stunned boys stumbling
in the long confusion of their lives toward

what one might call the edge *that is there
and always will be,* for three have already found it,
and the one who has not ponders the mathematics
of the spirit, and Ira Campbell, who found God there.

Les Passages

the arcades . . . are residues of a dream world.

—WALTER BENJAMIN

The piano player at Nordstrom's was crying,
and no one knew what to do. His hands were thin
and pale as the starched cuffs that seemed to hold
his wrists above the keyboard until they collapsed
and lay there among the ache of his sobs and awful
silences and the tapping of cash registers, the ocean
of small voices, the hum and click of commerce.

We all stood there, looking at him, then away,
fine linen trousers hanging from our arms,
or scent of cologne we could not afford thickening
the air, or right foot half-slipped into the new blue shoe
we would not buy, not now, not ever, and those stiff
little cries kept coming, kept tumbling across
that immense, gleaming floor into the change rooms

where men and women were gazing into mirrors
far from this strange sadness that fell clumsily
into a day rushing like all days on earth to fulfill itself,
to complete like the good postman its mission, and so
we paused in the crumbling silence until the fragile,
cautious tones of "Autumn Leaves" began to drift
through the aisles and around the glittering display cases

as if a dream, a great dream, were being dreamed again,
and the cries of an infant rose now from the other end
of the mall, cries bursting into screams and then one long
scream that spread its wings and lifted, soaring,
and we grew thoughtful and began to move about again,
searching our pockets, wallets, purses, tooled leather
handbags for something that would stop that scream.

Wittgenstein, Dying

Someone who, dreaming, says, "I am dreaming," even if
he speaks audibly in doing so, is no more right than if
he said in his dream, "it is raining," while it was in fact
raining. Even if his dream were actually connected
with the noise of the rain.

—*ON CERTAINTY*, NO. 676, WRITTEN ON HIS DEATHBED

The way a sentence is a story. *It is raining.*
Something happens, as the case may be, to something
of a certain kind and in a certain way.
*Im Aufang war die Tat. In the beginning was
the act.* So I tell a story: *it is raining.*
Grammar as a mirror of the world. Poor Trakl,
without a world except the world of words beyond
mere speech, drenched with dreams I never understood.
War, the nightmare of the earth, while in my backpack
Tolstoy's *Gospel* preached belief's old dream. I said,
once, *The sense of the world must lie outside the world.*
If that sense is "God," we might stand in His *rain,*
in "belief" of Him, but cannot quite get wet from it.
It is raining. In this room, the fire is blackening
the hearth's old stones, the now of my observing it
the only heaven of the mind. I said in my dream,
it is raining, but I dreamed the words themselves
and even that the words have meaning. Nonsense, then,
though now the rain is spattering the sixteen panes,
four by four, of my window. Keats, dying, looked out
a window at the Spanish Steps, Rome dimming in
the rain to gauzy nothing that must have seemed a dream,

like Madeline in his poem on St. Agnes' Eve.
Porphyro lying next to her spoke himself *into*
her dream, the voice she heard as *known* as the hand
of Moore showing the other one exists: "Here is one hand."
Because all certainty at least *begins* with the body's
certainty. My brother, Paul, playing Brahms,
feels his amputated arm, his hand, still moving.
Can the body *know?* Can, therefore, the mind?
Thought is the mind minding, poetry the mind
embodied, what cannot be spoken, that is, *explained:*
these curtains—Burano lace, I think—that sift
the April light, walls papered with lurid rose designs,
a bird in the window's lower panes resting on
a branch. In Ireland, chaffinches feeding
from my hand. With what certainty! "Here is one
hand." *It is raining.* And if I say, *I am dying,*
within this finite life enclosed at either end
by the unknowable, what are my words—
not a knowing, surely, but a kind of wonder
bodied forth here where the Cambridge rain comes down
on Storeys Way in a house called Storeys End.

The Barber

The barber shaves all and only men who do not
shave themselves. Who shaves the barber?

—BERTRAND RUSSELL'S PARADOX

I have been waiting so long . . . little pocks
of rust freckle the shanks of my best blades.
Who, after all, would be shaved by a barber
boasting foliage of such grotesque proportions,
dragging its damp, heavy life along sidewalks
and alleyways, doomed to this eternal algebra
of existence, these parallel universes
of paradox where bearded and beardless
coexist simultaneously and separately
and my twin in his timeless moment stands
mirrored in the lather of despair, blade
scraping flesh forever barren. Between us:
nothing, a space infinite and infinitesimal,
the sunless, silent arctic zone of contradiction.
On my side Cretans always lie; on his,
the lies are always true. On my side, particles;
on his, waves. A life unimaginable, but a life.

My wife—anguished, disgusted—long since done
with making love to Sherwood Forest, amused
herself with knitting it into increasingly
bizarre shapes, single rope ladders at first,
then interconnected hair suits for a trio
of monkeys. She lives in Alexandria now

with a Greek financier, a balding man of pink,
pampered countenance who offered me thousands
to shave. He sympathized. He saw in me the fate
of the common world lugging its debts and losses
through the streets like a black beard of shame,
the clean face of prosperity ever disappearing
until the man disappears, a walking shadow,
a beard bearing a man, a man engulfed
in the chaos of his own flesh, his own hair.

The razor strops of fate hang uselessly
beside their cruel mirrors. Among the dazzle
of chrome embellishments, bottles of Wildroot
and cans of Rose Pomade cry *Traitor!*
to my lank tresses, and old customers,
victims themselves of cut-rate solitudes
in downtown hotels, wander by with lowered eyes
and trembling hands. Shaggy children gawk
and scatter when they spy in the shop's
deep shadows a chair of hair, a breathing mound
multiplied infinitely in mirrors facing mirrors.

My only solace is a dream, a tonsorial fantasy
that more and more possesses me, of a world
in which the calculus of being demands that
barbers shave only men who shave themselves.

In it my twin and I stand handsomely behind
our chairs, he sporting a small goatee,
my nude visage chaste as an egg, immaculately
conceived, saintly in its pure nakedness,
and an entire cosmos of the newly shaven,
redolent with lotions but somehow needing
our final caresses and fleshly blessings,
lines the boulevard. The sun is shining.
The brick streets glow richly. And beside me
my wife prepares the secret oils of anointment
and reaches up to stroke my silken chin.

Hume

for Peter Caws

> . . . experience only teaches us, how one event constantly
> follows another; without instructing us in the secret
> connexion, which binds them together, and renders them
> inseparable.
>
> —DAVID HUME,
> *AN ENQUIRY CONCERNING HUMAN UNDERSTANDING*

Philosophia: declining Kansas light
lifting dust motes from the shadows, scars
along the prewar plaster walls of Fraser Hall.
Professor Caws, left hand raised against the sun,
right hand mapping on the board each turn
and pivot in Hume's argument against
causality. Hume's game, like mine,
is pool: one ball strikes another, and between
the two, says Caws, *nada,* nothing but
coincidence. And forget the thousand times
it happens, that little sad inductive leap.
I'm stunned. A, then B. And between them, what,
some vast, flat plain of pure event where things
just happen—a bird falling from the sky,
a distant shout, a cow wandering along
the highway's shoulder, the sun here, then there,
the moon full or empty, a white boat floating
on a sea of wheat.
                    That's it: a sea between
two countries: the land of *Cause,* like Iceland,

clean, uncluttered, a kind of purple mist
hanging in the air, a few cold souls caught
in midstride on a frozen lake, the awful silence,
trees that fall without a sound, and across the bay,
Effect, marching bands in every street,
unruly crowds, that balmy island climate,
and the thick, melodic accents of its citizens
that make you think of Istanbul, or wine,
or tile floors in geometrical designs—
and in between, the sea, soundless but for
the crash of waves, since nothing happens there
except the constant passage, back and forth,
of the little boat called the Logic of Induction
that never reaches shore. And there it is
in the distance—listing, it seems to me—
its pilot, nameless and alone, slumped
across the wheel.
                    Walking out of class,
breathing in the cold, salt air of Hume,
I turn to Anderson, our point guard:
"You no-talent hack, you're just a servant
of coincidence. Take that to the NBA."
"I'll drink to that," he says, and so we head
for Duck's, a game of pool, and look across
that flat green field, listening to the click
and thump of billiard balls, studying

the angles, as our ignorant young lives
pass slowly like the evening sun, unmoved,
unmoving, that sinks below the Kansas plain.

Gödel

So here is Campbell, murky, shadow-blotched
beneath the backroom table lamp at Duck's,
first one of us to dig past proposition 4.2
in the *Tractactus,* Dante's true disciple,
unfurling long verbal tapestries by heart
from *Purgatorio* (the dullest parts,
perversely), Cutty Sark in hand, always,
it seemed to me, in darkened rooms—scarred,
name-carved booths in downtown college bars,
jazz joints in Kansas City where after Reed
and the Sorbonne he played lounge piano
at the Muehlbach, claimed to know the mob
("'double-entry bookkeeping,' Lansky said,
'was Western culture's breakthrough'"), argued
Plotinus held the key to quantum mystery,
Gödel's madness proved the end of thought.

The end of thought! And then the cosmic sweep
of hands, smile's exploding nova, eyes two moons
across that smoke-burdened, blue neon room—
a kind of storm, or far, Cartesian weather.
Shapeless forms balloon inside a lava lamp
above the Wurlitzer's warped, ancient Coltrane,
"Body and Soul"—"the music of *becoming,*"
Campbell says, "Plato's spiral of ascent
toward the Forms, the unattainable,

the way those chords unravel, then take flight . . ."
His voice wobbles, trails off, vanishes
beneath the gathering cloud of his cigar,
then floats back up, "Gödel, you see, had proved
no system is complete or closed, no life
contains its own clear validation." Arms
waving, he heads back into the kitchen
where he washes dishes now and lives
behind the Texaco across the street, among
his books, and thinks about the end of thought.

FROM
*The Beauty of
Abandoned Towns*

In memory of O.T. and Nellie Swearingen

. . . labor omnia vicit
improbus et duris urgens in rebus egestas.

—VIRGIL, *GEORGICS*

1. The Beauty of Abandoned Towns

> Finally we sold out—you know, the big farm eats
> the small farm.
>
> —EDNA PFORR, NORTH DAKOTA

> ... ruins do not speak; we speak for them.
>
> —CHRISTOPHER WOODWARD, *IN RUINS*

Jefferson, Marx, and Jesus. Looking back, you can hardly believe it.

Bindweed and crabgrass shouldering through asphalt cracks, rats scuttling down drainpipes, undergrowth seething with grasshoppers.

The bumper crop in 1929. I stood on the front porch, dawn rolling over me like a river baptism because I was a new man in a new world, a stand of gold and green stretching from my hands to the sun coming up. In a way, a mirage. We bought a house in town. There it is. Or was.

The water tower, taller than the copper domes of Sacred Heart in Leoville, silhouette flooding the football field, missing boards of the scavenged bleachers, minor prophecies: *Bobby + Pam forever, Panthers rule, PEACE NOW.*

Presence is absence, says the philosopher. The future devours the past. Look at the goatgrass and ragweed claiming the feed store.

Sunflowers banging their heads on a conclusion of brick, the wind's last argument lost in a yellow cloud.

Eugene Debs set up The People's College in Fort Scott. Meridel Le Sueur grew up there. It lasted three years. Imagine: Comrade Debs, Comrade Sheppard, Comrade Le Sueur. In Kansas.

The open windows of the high school no longer surprise, pigeons flying in and out, the dumb cry of blackboards, wooden desks hauled away with the carved names of the long absent, the lost, the dead, the escaped.

The Farmer's Alliance tried. Socialist farm policy was for them a straight road to Jefferson's democracy. But they were always blocked by the big landowners. The deal breaker was profits, not politics. The harvest was topsoil, not wheat.

The last hitching post. The last horse, I suppose. Like Sunday morning, the last hymn, the last person to hear the last hymn. *May the circle be unbroken.* The circle is broken.

We subscribed to the Haldeman-Julius Appeal to Reason, *published out of little Girard, Kansas. Our children grew up on his Little Blue Books. The Federalist Papers, Thoreau, Emerson, Marx, Ingersoll, Upton Sinclair.*

The clapboard stores, slats long ago sand-blasted in dust storms, bleached or ochre now, gray, the faint green and yellow of a Lipton Tea ad on red brick. Broken windows flashing the setting sun in a little apocalypse of light, blind men in shades staring at the horizon, waiting for a sign. Stillness everywhere.

You know, you're wasting your time. No one gives a shit about this. None of it. No one.

Dearth of cars, motion, grind of gears, noise of commerce, chatter and cry of farm kids dangling from the beds of rusted-out pickups, murmur and guffaw of old men outside the Savings and Loan, stories, jokes. Quiet as a first snow. Somewhere a dog barks. A wire gate slams shut.

I'm so goddamned old I still tense up when an afternoon sky darkens. A roller would come in, dust up to eight thousand feet. If you were in the field, you were lost until it cleared. Or dead from suffocation. Where was your family? Where were your children?

Houses with tin roofs, wrap-around porches for watching thunderstorms, most vacant but here and there pickup windows flaming in sunset, trimmed lawn, history in forty years of license plates nailed to the garage wall. Cellar door. Swing set, that little violin screech of rusted chains, hush of evening, choir of cicadas. The living among the dead.

It started when agriculture professors began to teach farming as a business rather than a vocation. And then the big ones over the years ate the little ones. But in this country vocations are exploited. Ask the public school teachers.

The lords of grain: two cats fat on field mice lounge beneath the elevator steps where dust from a caliche road powders them white—wraiths, or white surrender flags.

On the other hand, subsidies can kill small farms these days. Back then we were desperate. Our children were hungry. FDR kept us alive. Then something went wrong. Big got bigger, small died. Still dying, hanging on but bedridden. The Ogallala Aquifer's almost tapped out. I mean, for God's sake.

Between the boarded bank and the welding shop husks drift like molted feathers or the sloughed scales of cottonmouths. Weeds waist-high shade the odd shoe still laced, a Coke carton bleeding into bluestem, dulled scraps of newsprint that say who died in Ashland or Sublette or Medicine Lodge.

It goes back to the oikos, the Greek family farm. Some ethic, some code of honor, kept them small. Big was vulgar, immoral. The Romans, too. Cato the Elder, rich as Joe Kennedy, taught his son agronomy, not commerce.

They are not haunted. They are not the "ghosts of themselves." They are cousin to vanishing, to disappearance. They are the highway that runs through them.

The picture show shut down decades ago. That's where we saw the world, the world our children and grandchildren ran off to. What happens when a nation loses its agrarian populace? My grandson worked as an usher there. He's a poet now. We have more poets than farmers. I don't think that's what Jefferson had in mind.

Not even decline, but the dawn of absence. Architecture of the dead. The lives they housed are dust, the wind never stops.

A disproportionate percentage of the American soldiers killed in Iraq were from small rural towns. The farmer/soldier, foundation of the Greek polis. *Fodder for war. Blood harvest.*

The wind never stops. *Our children were hungry.* The highway's long blade under the sun. *Something went wrong.* The towns are empty. *The circle is broken.*

2. Bloom School

In 1936 dust storms would clot
the mortar of its bricks, but now the wind
sweeps clean its crumbling, fluted columns
and pollinates a field of bluestem
and sunflowers tall as high school kids.
Nothing is everywhere: doorless doorways,
dirt-filled foundations, and weed-pocked
sidewalks leading to a sky that blued
the eyes of bored students stupefied
by geometry and Caesar's Latin.

Gallia est omnis divisa in partes tres.
Who cared how Gaul's past was divvied up?
Every radio in every car in Bloom
cried *Now,* and now was an eternity
except at graduation when the future
was invented by the Baptist minister.
The stars that evening fell on Main Street
and sank into our laminated hoods
streaked with downtown lights, and heaven
once more rolled across our rolling lives.

My wife and I made love here last night.
I manage kitchenware at Walmart,
and sometimes the future rides my back the way
I rode my rented combine years ago.

So Ann and I will come here evenings when
a fat moon floats in absent hallways, their lost,
remembered voices rising through the stillness,
and in other rooms students struggle over
Euclid's arcs and circles and bend to translate
the vanished past into another tongue.

3. The Teller

The bank so buried under hungry shrubs,
snakeweed, and creeper reaching even
to the carved stone BANK ESTABLISHED 1910
that its octagonal rust brick seems to shirk
a street long gone.
                        Where is he now,
Mr. Spivey, the only teller, who lived
above STATE FARM and had a wife in Blue Creek
he never saw? What led him there?
What kept her in a darkness we could
only wonder at? Men lived with wives,
we thought, the new moon rose, snow fell,
and familiar as a thumb each Sunday
Mr. Spivey sang the solo parts in choir,
angelically, our mothers said.
                        Fridays,
staying late, he cashed our paychecks,
small hands counting out and pushing
stacks of new bills crisp as corn sheaves
beneath the cage. Smiling through the bars,
he called us *mister,* as I, oddly, call him now.
Good evening, Mr. Elwood. Good day, Mr. Smith,
the words thin and lyrical as the paper
whispering in our ears.
                        Coming from the PALACE
those nights, we would sometimes see his shadow

in the risen window on the square, the streets
of Edward Hopper dimly lit below where
people walked and laughed and talked
about new money earned and saved or spent.
All across America there must have been
such streets and such men who touched
the people's hands with money and lived alone.

4. Wheat

For in the night in which he was betrayed,
he took bread.

In Clyde, Missouri, the Benedictine Sisters
of Perpetual Adoration cut unleavened bread
into communion wafers and gather them

in plastic bags folded, stapled, and later packed
in boxes. After compline the sisters rise again
from prayers, lie down upon their narrow beds,

and wait for sleep's wide wings to fold around them.
Their hands still give the light sweet smell of bread,
and loaves like little clouds drift through their dreams,

wafers raining down to make a blizzard
of the Word made flesh, *Corpus Christi,*
of God's own Son. On evening break at Walmart

Doris Miller spreads ketchup on her Big Mac
and salts her fries, time and wages swallowed
like a sacrament, eternity the dregs

that throng and cluster in the shallows
of her complimentary Styrofoam cup.
At the Exxon next door, Walter Miller

lifts his pickup's hood, then turns to stare
at the acreage he used to own across the road.
Was his wheat, he wonders, even the smallest grain

in its long ascent to final form, ever changed into
the body of our Lord? The Benedictine Sisters
of Perpetual Adoration wake to matins, prayers

that rise like crane migrations over feedlots,
packing houses, hog farms, the abandoned small
stores of Leeton, the Dixon Community Center,

the Good Samaritan Thrift Shop in Tarkio.
A gravel road veers toward the Open Door Cafe,
windows boarded up and painted powder blue

and lemon Day-Glo, perpetual sunrise on
a town silent as the absent cry of starlings
or idle irrigation pumps rusting in the dust

of August, where the plundered, corporate earth
yields the bread placed in the outstretched palms,
take and eat, of the citizens of Clyde, Missouri.

Madonna and Child, Perryton, Texas, 1967

A litter of pickups nose into Sancho's Market
south of town late Friday night rinsed in waves
of pink neon and samba music from some station
in Del Rio spilling out across the highway.
Sancho's wife dances alone behind the cash box
while her daughter, Rosa, tries to quiet her baby
whose squalls rip through the store like a weed cutter
shredding the souls of the carnal, the appetitious,
indeed the truly depraved as we in our grievous
late-night stupor and post-marijuana hunger
curse the cookie selection and all its brethren
and Al yells at Leno lost among the chips,
beef jerky, string cheese, *bananas* for Chrissakes,
that if he doesn't stop now and forever telling
Okie jokes he will shoot his dog who can't hunt
anyway so what the hell, but the kid is unreal,
a cry ascending to a shriek, then a kind
of rasping roar, the harangue of the gods,
sirens cleaving the air, gangs of crazed locusts
or gigantic wasps that whine and ding our ears
until the air begins to throb around us
and a six-pack of longnecks rattles like snakes
in my hand. And then poor Rosa is kissing
its forehead, baby riding her knee like a little boat
lost at sea, and old Sancho can't take it either,
hands over his ears, *Dios mio, ya basta! Dios mio,*

so Rosa opens her blouse, though we don't look,
and then we do, the baby sucking away, plump cheeks
pumping, billowing sails of the *Santa Maria*
in a high wind, the great suck of the infinite
making that little *nick, nick* sound, Rosa
smiling down, then Sancho turns off the radio
and we all just stand there in the light and shadow
of a flickering fluorescent bulb, holding
our sad little plastic baskets full of crap,
speechless and dying a little inside as Rosa
whispers *no llores, no llores, mija, mijita,*
no llores, and the child falls asleep, lips
on breast, drops of milk trickling down,
we can even hear it breathing, hear ourselves
breathing, the hush all around and that hammer
in our chests so that forty years later
this scene still hangs in my mind, a later work,
unfinished, from the workshop of Zurbarán.

What He Said

When Candi Baumeister announced to us all
that J.D. was *in love* with Brigitte Bardot,
drawing those two syllables out like some kid
stretching pink strands of Dubble Bubble
from between her teeth, J.D. chose not
to duck his head in the unjust shame
of the truly innocent but rather lifted it
in the way of his father scanning the sky
in silent prayer for the grace of rain abundant
upon his doomed soybeans or St. Francis
blessing sparrows or the air itself, eyes radiant
with Truth and Jesus, and said, *Babydoll,*
I would walk on my tongue from here to Amarillo
just to wash her dishes.
                         There is a time
in the long affliction of our spoken lives when,
among all the verbal bungling, stupidity,
and general disorder that burden us
like the ragged garment of the flesh itself, when,
beneath the vast and articulate shadows
of the saints of language, the white dove of genius
with its quick, wild wings has entered our souls,
our immaculate ignorance, and we are,
at last, redeemed. And so is conceived and born
the thing said, finally, *well*—nay, *perfectly*—
as it might be said by that unknowable Being

for whom we have in our mortal linguistic incapacity no adequate name except the one Candi Baumeister bore in her own virginal moment of absolute poetry: *My God, J.D.*

FROM
*Five Prose Poems
from the Journals
of Roy Eldridge Garcia*

Cendrars

Blaise, Maria, and I were walking toward the Seine from his apartment on the rue Montaigne, and he was speaking of Apollinaire, Captain Lacroix, Abel Gance, and others, his planned biography of Mary Magdalene, his beloved son, Remy, whose plane was shot down in WWII, Blaise's experience in WWI, the loss of his right arm. And he mentioned the phantom limb sensation, the pain of it, as if the arm were still there, that it is like memory, the memory that will not quite go away, that it is in effect the body's memory, but more, that is like poetry, the phantom life: not there in any material way, yet intensely there to the reader, the amputee who has lost some nameless yet essential limb of existence, probably on the long, dark path out of childhood. Teary-eyed with excitement, the reader can say of the poem, *yes, this is *life,* or better, this is the life *within* life, but try to convince the passerby, the onlooker, who will simply observe the empty sleeve flapping in the wind and shake his head sadly. Then he returned to his favorite subject, the levitation of saints, much as he had spoken of it in *Le Lotissement du ciel* years before, and Paris rose around us as if for the first time—the sun like the oranges of the surrealists plunging into the Seine, the wild applause of the chestnut trees, the truncated towers of Notre Dame—and Maria looked at me and smiled that odd, worried smile that is still with me. Whose pain will not leave. A plane falling out of the sky. That phantom smile.

Aix-en-Provence, 1952

Piano

The blind piano tuner had come to the wrong address. I said, "I'm very sorry. You must have the wrong address." He insisted on seeing the piano, though I have none. I showed him the living room, which was being recarpeted. "A Bösendorfer! Wonderful! One of the finest! What an opportunity!" He was overjoyed, talking at length about its virtues, second to none—the crisp, clean tone, silken touch, huge bass, marvelous sustain, and so forth. He took out his tuning kit and began immediately. He claimed to have heard Schnabel play the entire Beethoven sonata cycle on one in Royal Albert Hall in London. After a short time, he played a chord. "Hear that? Wonderful. So rich." I told him I could hear nothing, and he nodded sympathetically, even sadly, saying that to lose one's sense of hearing was to lose a portion of one's soul. "In his last days, Beethoven heard with his fingertips, I truly believe that," he muttered to himself. To hear him soliloquize rhapsodically about the piano and the great performers he had heard—"Hoffman with his small hands would have loved this light action, like angel wings," or "Perfect for Lipatti and his Chopin, so fluid and transparent"—was almost to hear the music itself, to be seated in the concert hall, center of the third row, to feel the tremble of the young woman's shoulder in the adjacent seat, her barely repressed sighs in the crescendos of the *Appassionata,* that unearthly, mystical moment between the dying of the last note and the avalanche of applause. His devotion to the Bösendorfer, the obsessive attention to every detail of the tuning process, preoccupied him for most of the afternoon, and I served him coffee, then afterward offered him a martini in celebration of a job well done. "You're a lucky man, such a fine instrument," he said, as if to the piano itself, as he left. Yes I am, I thought, and looked back at the living room the way Beethoven must have looked at that young woman in the third row, her tear-filled eyes, the slightly parted lips, her hands pressed together as if in prayer.

Los Angeles, 1957

Moth

A moth devoured words.

—THE EXETER BOOK

A larval tunneling between pages.
    Gorged on print,
wallowing in pulp, it falls into the long

sleep that later breaks and frays as wings
    sluggish as oars
begin to bludgeon the heavy air,

baffled by walls of dusk and lugging
    the soft body
toward a squall of light. Dun wings

flail, ribbed like Gothic vaults and
    camouflaged with moons
large as owl eyes. Lurching through

the light's rain, it veers, collides,
    hugs the bulb
and falls away. And the singed antennae

recall in something like a mezzotint
    the larval dark passage,
the hunger, the gray dream of *with, and, the.*

Triptych:
Nathan Gold, Maria,
On the Waterfront

Nathan Gold

9/14/01. So, Sollie, here I am again, an old man,
zeyde, now. You're gone ten years, but it's your birthday
and I'm standing here as always on Brooklyn Bridge
and staring at that skyline, writing it all down.
The longest journey in this country, Uncle Mike
would say, *stretches from the Lower East Side to
the Upper East,* and weekends you would see them there,
the rich, the big shots, strolling to the Met, say,
or Guggenheim to see the Rembrandts or Chagalls,
gold flecks of light drifting down through leafy branches
to settle on the shoulders of their silk, tailored suits.
So I'm halfway: a three-room near the Chelsea, not bad,
considering what might have been. Some years ago
I ran into Reznikoff at Dubrow's on Seventh Ave.
when he was writing *Holocaust,* and he blurts out,
*Eichmann said his entire life was founded on
one moral principle: Kant's categorical imperative,
later modified for the "small man's household use."*
My God, can you believe it? Food spewed from his mouth,
his hands were shaking. *Thousands murdered everyday.*
He read Kant and yet. . . . Language rendered useless.
Thought turned inside out. Rez wrote his poems true to fact
but often with a sense of failure. Three days ago
I knew this sense, words failing, as the towers drowned
in smoke, as the *Malach HaMavet* spread its wings
across the city. Rabbi Stern, a good man, a holy man,

prayed in its shadow, bewildered as the rest of us.
And so, Crane's poem, *Under thy shadow by the piers*
I waited; Only in darkness is thy shadow clear . . .
but *lend a myth to God*? No, I don't think so. The wings
are spread too wide this time and stain the river gray
the way that Kansas dust storm turned the sky death-gray
when we were boys on our trip out west, hitchhiking.
All that space, all that American space Crane's bridge
embraced, and not just Brooklyn to Manhattan, but coast
to coast, *Vaulting the sea, the prairies' dreaming sod.*
And he should be here now as I am, groping for
the words, the true ones, for a country and a city
like none anywhere whose streets are shrouded gray
(some days, Mike said, near Lublin it came down
like snow, like *snow*), whose skies are ruined with ash.

Maria

Maria Rasputin, b. 1899, Siberia; d. 1977,
Los Angeles, California

They say the fortress has been taken; it is evening,
it is dark, rebelling horseguards just went past with
music. Autos race along Zagródny without cease; they
are met with shouts of "Hurrah!" Soldiers and workers
shoot into the air, there are few people out, it is noisy and
dark; soldiers roam around in groups, smoke, and shoot
aimlessly. The revolution has taken the form of a military
uprising. . . . Chaos, forces of the century.

      —*THE DIARIES OF NIKOLAY PUNIN*, 1917

A circus. Circles. Everything comes round, Pyotr.
May I call you Pyotr? I knew so many then.
Look up there, the freeway, cars trunk to tail like
circus elephants. Feed them or they'll trample you.
I know. Ringling Brothers. I trained animals,
but lions mostly. Yes. Almost killed once, a bear
in Indiana. Russia, Budapest. And Paris,
where I danced in cabarets, then New York, later
Florida, now L.A. A riveter in Long Beach,
but too old now, I babysit for the bourgeois rich,
and when they ask for my credentials, I say,
I babysat the daughters of the Czar of Russia.
That shuts them up. You're too polite, of course, to ask
about my father. "Mad Monk," indeed. I don't know,
the women, that crazy cult. And God knows I'm no saint
myself. But all past. Long time. Vodka under the bridge.
He was my father, and he loved me. History

judges him, nothing I can do. Listen: *history
is a mess, just one damned thing and then another.*
Believe me, I know. *I was there.* The door of history
closes, opens. It opened, I went through. Czar,
Czarina, children, gone. Varya, Mitia, gone.
All gone. And I survive. Two husbands, five countries,
two wars, and look, I'm here talking to Blake scholar,
yes? Blake, the one with visions, angels, yes? You come
to study in the mansion of the Railroad King.
The bourgeois rich. My father had a vision and told
Czar Nicholas, *Don't go to war. It's Serbia,
not our affair.* Everything comes round. Pyotr,
you say your father fought in World War Two. The mess
of history being what it is, does it not amaze you,
but for a little man named Wilhelm with a withered arm,
a tiny brain, and a Germany to play with,
there might not have been a First World War, a vengeful peace,
an Adolf, another war, and you, like thousands more,
without a father? *They murdered mine.* Mad, maybe,
but he told him twice. Or that if the Archduke's idiot
driver had turned right instead of left, then no
assassination, no *Great War,* and decades later,
no absent fathers. Maybe. *But he had a vision!
He knew!* History is a mess: whatever we do now,
a hundred years from now they're burying the victims.
Bozhe moi. In Paris, just before I left, there was

a man named Kojève whose idea was *the end*
of history, and *desire,* the little engine running it.
Intellectuals in the cabarets would speak of it.
(What did I know? Like you, I come from peasants.
I just listened.) And in Ringling Brothers, something
called a *freak show,* was a little girl named Frieda Pushnik
with only half a body. Intelligent, so brave,
a soul, no arms to push against the world, no legs
to run away from it. Well, I'm a freak of history,
I thought. She can do it, so can I. And so I did.
So, Pyotr, look again. Up there. The freeway, trunk
to tail like circus elephants. And who will feed them?
Who will they trample to get more? There's your *desire,*
your *want,* and trust me, it is endless. But the end
of history? Oh no, Pyotr. It's only just begun.

On the Waterfront

know thyself

Flashlight in hand, I stand just inside the door
in my starched white shirt, red jacket nailed shut
by six gold buttons, and a plastic black bowtie,
a sort of smaller movie screen reflecting back
the larger one. *Is that really you?* says Mrs. Pierce,
my Latin teacher, as I lead her to her seat
between the Neiderlands, our neighbors, and Mickey Breen,
who owns the liquor store. Walking back, I see
their faces bright and childlike in the mirrored glare
of a tragic winter New York sky. I know them all,
these small-town worried faces, these natives of the known,
the real, a highway and brown fields, and New York
is a foreign land—the waterfront, unions, priests,
the tugboat's moan—exotic as Siam or Casablanca.
I have seen this movie seven times, memorized the lines:
Edie, raised by nuns, pleading—praying, really—
Isn't everybody a part of everybody else?
and Terry, angry, stunned with guilt, *Quit worrying*
about the truth. Worry about yourself, while I,
in this one-movie Kansas town where everyone
is a part of everybody else, am waiting darkly
for a self to worry over, a name, a place,
New York, on 52nd Street between the Five Spot
and Jimmy Ryan's where bebop and blue neon lights
would fill my room and I would wear a porkpie hat
and play tenor saxophone like Lester Young, but now,

however, I am lost, and Edie, too, and Charlie,
Father Barry, Pop, even Terry because he worried
more about the truth than he did about himself,
and I scan the little mounds of bodies now lost even
to themselves as the movie rushes to its end,
car lights winging down an alley, quick shadows
fluttering across this East River of familiar faces
like storm clouds cluttering a wheat field or geese
in autumn plowing through the sun, that honking,
that moan of a boat in fog. I walk outside
to cop a smoke, *I could have been a contender,*
I could have been somebody instead of . . . what I am,
and look across the street at the Army-Navy store
where we would try on gas masks, and Elmer Fox
would let us hold the Purple Hearts, but it's over now,
and they are leaving, *Goodnight, Mr. Neiderland,*
Goodnight, Mrs. Neiderland, Goodnight, Mick, Goodnight,
Mrs. Pierce, as she, a woman who has lived alone
for forty years and for two of those has suffered through
my botched translations from the Latin tongue, smiles,
Nosce te ipsum, and I have no idea what she means.

New Poems

The Story

It has no name and arrives from nowhere,
eager for new adventures: the murmur and cries
of the crowded streets of Istanbul or Rome
or Brooklyn, the blazing eyes of the last gray wolf
deep in a cave in New Mexico, the sob of the wind
between the disks of an abandoned tractor
on the high plains, the homeless man chasing
his runaway grocery cart down Sunset Boulevard,
a young woman looking out from the front porch
of a duplex in Enid, Oklahoma, waiting for the mail.

It has, as they say, a mind of its own, bearing
secret knowledge, truths from another world,
transparent and untranslatable, luminous
and cryptic. It arrives almost silently, only
the slight crush of lawn grass beneath its sandals,
a surprise even though you have somehow
expected it. Your hands, rough and calloused
from the toils of the imagination, reach out
to gently shake its narrow shoulders, to tousle
its well-combed hair silvered by moonlight.
Where have you been? It says nothing, of course,
walks to the far corner of the room, and begins
to pray. After waiting for hours, you offer it
coffee and a slice of pecan pie, then more coffee.
When it leaves, you follow close behind in fear

and a traveler's anxiety. *Where can a story end?*
If it arrives from nowhere, where can it end?

But then, as you pass through familiar streets,
past the clapboard houses, the pomegranate tree
just coming into bloom, the blue Buick parked
by the curb, you understand, for there is your mother
among the bird cries of the porch swing, reading
a letter from a small island somewhere in the Pacific.
There is the front door with its torn screen,
the voices of a soap opera from the radio, the creak
and whisper of cottonwood branches overhead.
This is where the story ends. And now you know,
this is also where it begins, and you lean
into the light, put the pen to paper, and write.

Red Snow

A howling fluorescent dream car skids off
the highway, and I wake wracked by the fumes
of sleep's endless traffic, stumbling into morning,
night terrors with their long nails at my back.
A fury of splayed branches overhead rakes

the dawn light and claws the windowpanes.
That crazed windshield I woke to as a boy
stares out of the wreckage, radio snarling,
horn stuck, my mother's face veiled
in what seemed to be little glass stars or red snow.

Walking the hall. Dragging it all behind me
in the same sad robe I have worn now
nine years to breakfast. Trepidation's rags,
grim uniform of the land of dread,
the country of forgetting. Cheerios, sliced bananas.

Bad dreams. What could be more common?
Oh, I had such a bad dream. Good morning,
I've just been to hell, pour me some orange juice.
One wakes to the world. Where is my mother?
Where is my father? *I am not myself.*

The Left Fielder's Sestina

Ebbets Field, 1946

I lose it in the sun sometimes, a rain
of light, spray of shrapnel in my eyes,
flamethrowers cutting through the dark.
Then suddenly the ball finds shadows nailed
across the outfield wall glamorous with signs:
the SCHAEFER beer and CAMELS of the lost.

Lost because they've never known the truly lost:
the bodies floating pink with blood and rain
as we waded in, rifles held like little signs
above our heads, the dead with nightmare eyes
burning into ours. When I dream of nailing
triples high against the wall and wake to dark

hotel rooms, I see them there, lying dark
as waves along the beach that night we lost
the whole platoon except for three of us nailed
flat beneath barbed wire and a heavy rain
of cannon fire. Smart pitchers know the eyes
will sometimes give away the batter, sure signs

of hitter's lust, to break a slump, ignore the sign
from third, waive the bunt. An Okie kid the darkest
night on Guam told me this, death swimming in his eyes
and like me sick our best years of ball were lost

to the bloody goddamned war. That night the rain
stopped. A suicide attack, and we were almost nailed

to Hirohito's cross. Shrapnel flew like nails,
and I collapsed, a kind of seizure, bawling, signs
the war was stuck inside my brain, the pink rain
that never stops. *The dead.* The endless dark.
A coma is a house of dreams. You're lost
in it, no doors or windows, but then your eyes

one day open to the world again, the eyes
of thousands staring down, and those glass nails
of blinding sunlight as you take one deep, lost
in a kind of baseball heaven. The signs
along left field say, WELCOME HOME. The darkest
dreams begin to fade. Happiness comes down like rain.

Lightning strafes the sky. The batter eyes the sign
from first and nails his right cleat to the ground. Dark
clouds loom. We'll lose at home. To rain. *Sweet rain.*

Betty

Among azaleas and drooping lilies of the Nile
fagged from August's firestorm, Betty rakes
blown trash, groaning underneath the burdens
of a life of housework, teaching high school Latin,
and lugging one day to the next the heavy stones
of worry: blind son, vanished husband, taxes,
debt, and the Dodgers, who upset natural law
when they left Brooklyn for L.A. *It's all downhill,*
she yells to me across the yard, *you're not even you,*
and she quotes again the line from last night's *Nova:*
Every atom in your body was once inside a star.

Rising in a patch of autumn sunlight, she scans
her property: termite-ravaged fence, roof rats
gutting rotted oranges, tree roots buckling
the driveway, dry rot in the redwood planks,
crabgrass, clogged drains, her ancient bus on blocks,
UC Berkeley and peace-sign bumper stickers
from the sixties. Sunday morning she climbs in
with coffee, scones, and Seneca, her only saint.
Takes the metro to the track and puts down
ten on Trotsky's Dream. She likes the crowd,
hoi polloi, and *those horses beautiful as gods.*

Later, leaves tumble down on her diminished
form while she dozes in a plastic lawn chair

as if blind to seasons. But it's California,
green in winter and in September Santa Anas
swooping through the valley as Betty curses
the sudden news: liver cancer, her doctor says,
a month or two at most, and within a week
she's knocking on my door, mustard yellow,
death looming in her eyes. Tonight, 2 a.m.,
in moonlight I see someone standing in her yard:
Betty, beer in hand and staring at the stars.

The Game

Field lights that span the evening sky, siren songs
of kind, loud girls in thigh-high skirts, and then,
like a rush of cranes bruising the autumn silence,
the crowd leaping up and shouting as we stride
across that green plane bright with new lime
and dreams of high school immortality.

After the game, the old men buy us beer
and we drink it straight from pitchers held
like trophies, bronze in the neon light, foam
dribbling down our shirts. There is a sadness
in their happiness, their hands upon our backs.
We are their finest days now vanishing, or dead.

And so they buy a second round, a third,
for their brave young men. Ben White puts his fist
through drywall, and Timmy Doyle breaks
a pool cue with one hand. Undefeated,
drunk, in glory we drive home. We are heroes.
Our fathers scowl, our mothers tuck us into bed.

The Student Assistant

Across the street from Southwark Cathedral
after reaching nine centuries back to touch a wall
still standing through the London blitz where the sign
says, PLEASE DO NOT TOUCH. THIS WAS CONSTRUCTED
IN A.D. 1136, I walk the path a certain medical student
might have taken to Guy's Hospital in 1812 when
he was buying cadavers from the grave digger
at four in the morning as the heavy south bank fog
settled upon the shoulders of the Thames,
and having made his purchase in the surreptitious
thick night, dragging the corpse across cobbles
the way Hamlet *lugged the guts* of Polonius from
sudden vengeance into the murky halls of guilt.

This student assistant, a promising young man
with a brittle future and quick wit trudging through
the dingy film of the London night also wrote poems
about melancholy and the sweet, throbbing agony
of desire and beauty, but there he trod, pulling
his burlap sack over stone and muck and stair
with Southwark looming overhead like some dark god
of history, pulling death into the purgatorial rooms,
the terrifying, lye-washed, stinking, candlelit rooms
of Guy's Hospital. Little Keats. On his death trip.

History: Four Poems

1. Dust Storm, No Man's Land, 1952

First, the fluttering of screeching birds,
their sudden plunge and climb through manic,
spiral flights, chickens squawking in the backyard,
and then doors slamming and the air grieved
by gusts of prairie dirt as I look back
to see the sky turn sick with darkness,
a deep brown-green bile boiling up to smear
the sun dull as rusted-out tin siding
sinking now in muck, oblivion, the little
death of nightmares. I'm blind to my own body
and the vanished sidewalk where I crawl doglike
spooked by dead birds, the shock of feathers
to the touch, and scattered branches until
lighted windows begin to cleave the dust
the way a plow turns barren ground, the sod
I'm told that should have stayed unbroken,
ancient plains of short grass that fed bison
long before the massacres began. Home again,
I wake to silence like a newly fallen snow,
and in morning light a sheen as if dawn
were a kind of foil or bronze silk coverlet
lies across the room from bed to table
where a model plane has been painted gold
with sunlit dust and the floor holds brightness
the way the land itself must have one fine day

when they climbed down from their wagons
and smiled, for the wind was clean and the sky
was clear and they had come a very long way.

2. Shakespeare in the Park, 9/11/2011

Tonight beneath a Texas sky Lear wept
and gave his grief to a river in Fort Worth,
and an audience remembering the broken
towers of New York lay down their beers
and leaned into the dark. Shakespeare in a park
where not so long ago two thousand head
of cattle bound for slaughter grazed, stared
across America's frontier, and heard
the same cicadas' cry, its rise and fall.
Above Lear's absent crown the moon had paled
to little more than real estate where men
have walked. A poplar waved the stars away.
An army of cicadas sang the old mad song.

I will not sleep tonight. My children's children
breathe uneasily beneath the burden
of a story strange and not quite clear to them.
My wife dreams the passion of Cordelia
and the stupidity of men. Beyond
the lavish lawns and bushes of the higher
suburbs loom nightmares of a phony war.
Light will soon be moving on the plains,
and bare, forked animals will rise. As long
as the cicadas sing, I will not sleep tonight.

3. Economics

for the occupiers

We signed our names on their old papers. . . . We knew when
they cheated us out of every single little red cent. . . . We
knew that. We knew they were stealing. . . . We let them
think they could cheat us because we are just plain old
common everyday people. They got the habit.

—*WOODY GUTHRIE,* HOUSE OF EARTH

The teeming street, rich with crowds and voices,
huddled masses gleaming under rain and streetlights.
The human microphone, antiphonies of call, response,
and songs like ancient hymns among stone tombs
awakening once more the nocturnal gods of Wall Street.
And the old man's tale comes back to me outside
a long-abandoned bank in Oklahoma robbed in 1933
when locusts wedged between the sandstone bricks
throbbed their little desperation song, days on end
monotonous as rotting fence posts along dry fields,
the air a wall of dust, Black Bear Creek a bloodless scar,
and the horse people of the Otoe long since gone away.
His voice hardened into something thin and brittle
for *suddenly,* he said, *suddenly* back then, he knew,
in that flat Baptist land of bad deeds and worse money
where preachers raged against all forms of sin
except the greed of the sleeping kings of poverty,
that the scabby hand of vengeance was alive
and real and moving slowly through the fields
and burning streets of little towns like this one because

the third thief placed the barrel of his Remington
beneath the bank president's chin and said,
This, sir, is what happens when banks are built
on the broken backs of the people, while the young man
who became the old man who told this story lay
face down on the floor clutching his foreclosure notice
and thinking, *who is the thief here, who is the thief?*

4. Alzheimer's

When, when, when is what my sister mumbles now
beneath this tin-can piped-in music and parrots
squawking in the guest lounge, but what I see
is the light glancing from our mother's ring
as she hands the coins to the organ grinder
on the corner of Polk and Main one day in Houston,
1944, her face ruined, mascara running, the burden
heavy upon her, then later, the light crumbling
through the feverish leaves of cottonwoods
in the sideyard and still the sobbing, hands flailing,
that wobbly keening of the organ in my head,
those rickety tones floating up as if from an *island*
in the *Pacific* and next morning the coffee's perk
and bubble cluttering the air, the bacon's sputter,
a kind of chirping, I thought, of birds, Pacific ones,
and my father surely heard them since he was there
beneath those trees with leaves like big green hands
heaped with birds, *parrots,* for I had seen parrots
in a photograph from *Life* in all their brightness,
their grand carnival of yellow, red, and blue,
their coat-of-many-colors shapes against a beach
and the vast church choir of sky and cloud that rose
above it, and so that afternoon in Galveston
my mother looked across the waves that curl
and uncurl always, looking at the sea or toward
the far edge of the sea or beyond the sea, beyond

green islands or parrots or any of that as I showed
the photograph to my sister, saying this is where
our father is, where he's coming from, and my mother
grabbed it, crying *when, when, when, when, when.*

Three Girls Tossing Rings

Outside, the lawn slopes and billows under chestnut trees,
acres of pampered landscape floating in a limpid haze

that surrounds the house. Dressed in crinoline, white hose,
and flocks of ribbons, one of them tosses rings, the others

wait their turn behind the drapes of watered silk. A red ring
is thrown and misses, the yellow rims around the peg and stays.

No one keeps score. Their boredom is as natural as grass
and chestnut trees, or the dull advance of history from hill

to hill somewhere in the gray distances of Europe. A red ring,
a blue one, the arc the wrist makes in the throwing, the small feet

just so. Trenches hacked deep in the fields of another country,
holes where humans slept in mud, will green over, the broken limbs

of trees will flower, and the young girls tossing rings after Mass,
after the family meal, will turn and stroll across the wide, immaculate lawn.

The Death of a Gerbil

for Sarah

Small-bones, buried in a shallow grave,
black eyes now closed that led you through the night,
flat, drumming feet now stilled below the staves

my children crossed for you. You gave them light
on wet, dim weekends. And sick, asleep for days,
you taught them care, then grief. They made a rite

of solemn words and gestures meant to raise
you to some *paradiso,* the mind's embrace
of soft bodies, dark eyes, and unstained souls.

With this canto, mouse, *adieu.* Your sacrifice
was life encased in glass, or running through
their dreams pursued by fate's grim mask, the face

they woke up from but now must wake up to.
In those last days you held my children close,
then let them make a world, a grace, for you.

Pale from the Hand of the Child That Holds It

The bronze angel yawns among the photographs:
father and mother wearing the bright garments
of memory, that upended Eden where their lives
seem glamorous and sleek as Cadillacs in V-Day
parades, he in Navy whites, she in a wide-shouldered,
Joan Crawford fantasy of yellow explosions on a
blue field. Her dress ripples slightly at the hips
where his hands come to rest, and a chorus line
of date palms bends in unison behind them.
The dawn shadows of the room lap across son
and daughter, dreamily retouched in their robed
graduation portraits while over them looms
the enlarged family snapshot from Christmas.
Hearing the shutter snap like a plastic picnic fork
in the father's broad fist, they recalled summer
vacations laid out like cut flowers, the lake's shattered
calm, the charred hot dogs, bleached swimming trunks,
condoms nibbling at the peeling boat dock. Stamped
with the profile of some nameless Victorian,
the heirloom lamp squats in the table's center
as if this monument to domestic history could lift flesh
and blood from their chrome frames. And I, the son,
watch now how dust motes fall through lace curtains
like snow in one of those overturned glass balls
where a tree and house hang from a rounded meadow
above a sky pale from the hand of the child that holds it.

*Three Prose Poems
from the Journals of
Roy Eldridge Garcia*

An Attaché Case

One morning, only an hour after he arrived at the Bourse, M. Belperron, an *agent de change,* left his office, took a train to Deauville, and walked into the ocean, leaving his attaché case on the beach. The catatonic stillness of the attaché case affected everything. Was it just an object in the stream of events, soiled with the sweat of hands, wracked with an endless cycle of opening and closing, commercial documents placed inside, then removed, then reinserted? Or was it veering toward metamorphosis? These questions rolled over the beach in waves of such stunning tension that everything became fixed in its movements: the gulls fell and rose, the ocean pressed forward, then fell away, ripples of sand formed and vanished. The attaché case, too, felt itself yielding to the flow of the inevitable and began searching the horizon desperately, recalling the story M. Belperron loved to tell about Galileo inventing the telescope in order to see ships coming in before anyone else could, then quickly investing in their cargo and subsequently making a killing on the market. Soon a boat appeared, only a speck at first, but growing larger and larger. Opportunities were at hand. Someone needed to do something.

Aix-en-Provence, 1952

The End of Art

Raymone, Blaise, and I are in the Café de Flore arguing about Tolstoy's essay, "What Is Art?" and Raymone, in her excellent but occasionally imperfect English, says, "In his later years Tolstoy enjoyed walking around dressed as a *pheasant*." Raymone, I was wrong and you were right. There *was* something birdlike about him. Something feathery. Colorful. Exotic. And rather small. He hated the art of Shakespeare and Chekhov, as all pheasants do. They have these long tail feathers. Their art is in their ass, you might say. Tolstoy wanted to forget he was a count. Like Marie Antoinette at Versailles dressing up like a peasant in clothing of her own design and walking about in her little peasant village, where there were no peasants. Real cabbage and turnips and tomatoes, but no peasants. The real peasants were at the gates, starving and crying out for food, watching Marie walking around pretending to be them. She was closer to a pheasant than a peasant. Her art was in her ass, where one might also find Tolstoy's aesthetic principles. It all makes sense now.

Paris, 1953

The Language of the Future

A language has to be found . . .

—RIMBAUD

The language of the future had invaded the desert. Its colors were magnificent: rose, indigo, emerald green, an excruciatingly pale yellow, an orange pure and bright as a bird-of-paradise, other unnameable shades and hues running together, and a black so unyielding that it threatened to engulf whatever it touched. The animals welcomed the new language, inviting it into their lairs and tunnels in the rocks. They found in it not so much a warmth as a familiarity, as of something buried and forgotten and then recovered unexpectedly. Perhaps, they thought, this is the way their gods had spoken before the great silence. But the other inhabitants of the desert had become accustomed to the silence, woke to it each morning like a second sun, and so the new language, even though keeping a polite distance from their houses, vaguely disturbed them. "It's that purple nonsense along the edges," offered one. "No, no, it's the sick yellow that gets under my skin," said another. They could not agree, but when the night embraced the language, first one shade and then another, and commenced its dark song, they knew a change was coming. Sure enough, in the deep, thickening mauve of night they rose like sleepwalkers from their beds and began the exodus, covering their ears against the chorus that swelled around them.

Liberal, Kansas, 1960

Language

Elvin in agony: tonnage of a full body
slam, shoulder into gut, crunch of cartilage
and bone, or still black dot of a perfect
spiral thrown level in the flat, receiver
spun around, held, then ground against
the grass now turned to stone, a hip bruise
thickening from pink to burgundy, then black,
that cruel idyllic meadow ribbed with grave lime,
white arms of the goal posts cradling the sky.

But at night Elvin liked to drink, zoned into
the stereo's blue glow among piled laundry,
bottles, books, photos of his mother looking
like Dolores del Rio as she posed on the beach
or beneath an umbrella held by a grinning,
drenched Elvin. With John Prine, *mi primo, el poeta,*
he sang about the *hole in daddy's arm, where
all the money goes,* and we kept our distance,
knowing all he wanted was the bleak purity
of an empty, darkened room, that blue light
summoning him somewhere off the common path,
somewhere serene, undemanding, a little sad,
like the song itself, like something heard and felt
from far away, or like the *celestial trance*
in Isaacs's *Maria* that we read in Spanish class.

He brought his mother's language and
his father's name from a Texas border town
and could recite, drunk or sober, and usually
drunk, that poem by Machado that begins,

Si yo fuera un poeta
galante, cantaría
a vuestros ojos un cantar tan puro
como en el mármol blanco el agua limpia,

and ends, . . . *vuestros ojos tienen*
la buena luz tranquila,
la buena luz del mundo en flor, que he visto
*desde los brazos de mi madre un día.**

He loved the sound of it, *light, then heavy,*
then light, like rain, he said. Strange talk,
which we heard but did not *listen* to, like
the crowd's hunger, their murmur and cry
at games, or some sort of code or riddle

---

* "If I were a poet / of love, I would make / a poem for your eyes as clear / as the
transparent water in the marble pool. . . . Your eyes have / the calm and good
light of the blossoming world, that I saw / one day from the arms of my
mother."

spoken in a darkened corner of the bar,
a lover's veiled, whispered confession beyond,
as they say, translation.
                    But then someone said,
Enough of the mother tongue, Elvin, speak it in English,
and after the ambulance left with the guy bleeding
from both ears, we just sat quietly and drank
and let the mystery roll on, pour down, like rain
pelting chickens in the backyards of south Laredo,
gutters filled with children playing in the mud.

Though small, a beast. And those few times
he sacked the quarterback, looming over him
like a god in judgment, the jubilation,
the *chenga* this and *chenga* that, was a bit, well,
excessive, a little weird, madness bubbling
into childish glee, roaring, arms waving,
and it worried even us. *What the fuck is it*
with Elvin? we would say in wonder, fear,
and admiration.
                    Me gusta? You think
I like it? I don't like it, he once said,
shunning as always the easy comraderie
of boys at war. The last game, a loss,
was the worst: an implosion of brick and glass,
Elvin's *venganza*—forehead, fists, cleats pummeling

the locker doors, slung helmet nailing
the fullback, Bitsko, just behind the ear,
this whacked-out, unholy, purple rage
goading everyone to tie their shoes, fast,
Get the hell out, now, Jesus, he's lost it,
everyone splitting, stone silence even
from the coaches, just crazy Elvin screaming
to an abandoned locker room, cursing God
and all His saints, punching the block wall
of a world mute as concrete, and the blood trails
running to the drain were still there Monday.
Elvin in the hospital that night, singing,
luz del mundo en flor, que he visto
desde los brazos de mi madre un dia.

Adios, gringos, his words as he walked
toward the bus at season's end. Back to
Laredo, his mom, a job at the stockyards,
and whatever storm was raging in his head.
I don't know. You tell me. *Rain,* he said

Abandoned Grain Elevator

after a photograph by Sant Khalsa

Pausing here, the anchorites of grain:
woman, girl, a paper angel
seated on the elevator steps
where dust from a caliche road
whitens the woman's boots. The horizon
is their god of open spaces.
The angel mouths silent hymns
to pass the time the last workers
bore upon their backs.

Mice scuttle through the tool shed.
A JOHN DEERE sign rattles on its post.
Across the field, a wind-scoured house
still hugs the ground
someone's grandson disked
before the land was sold, before
the family moved to Kansas City.

Below the steps, farm cats doze in bunchgrass,
the angel lifts its wings,
and the girl takes up its song,
May the circle be unbroken,
by and by, Lord, . . . her voice lost
in the toiling winds that rouse

the sleeping earth,
then lay it back on the shoulders
of the highway that led them there.

The Men on Figueroa Street, Los Angeles, 1975

At 6 a.m. they gather like chattering housewives outside the Goodwill store
and wait for the latest shipment of women's wear to arrive.
They are larger, especially their hands, and happier, too,
than you had imagined, as if clothing were luck, or the hems of dresses
they so love to touch held money or the answer to their one secret prayer.

Close up, you see the shoulders hard and broad under silk,
and the strong forearms for lifting sofas or luggage.
Their talk is quick and clever, like the banter of co-eds
waiting for dates, or excited children whose father
has been away but has suddenly returned, arms filled with gifts.

Soon the yellow truck arrives, the truck
that says GOODWILL in big red letters, and they press closer,
making those cool, sexual sounds of anticipation.
When the doors open and the chrome racks are rolled into the alley,
they do not become the wolves you might expect but rather

stand shyly by with their hands raised slightly
as if waiting for permission. The way the clothes come into their hands
is memorable, like an athletic feat, the outstretched fingers
and then the ball suddenly, delicately, there. With the whispers
and rich commerce of blouses, skirts, and lingerie

passing deftly from one large hand to another,
it occurs to you, *they know each other's sizes,*

they come often, every Friday morning before the traffic and tourists,
before the homeless across the street have thrown off their newspapers
and risen to the tasks of the new day on Figueroa Street.

You leave then, and later, strolling back to your hotel,
you see them lounging in pools of blue neon,
laughing and singing bits of popular song while seated languidly
along the curb in feather boas and satin jackets with padded shoulders.
And as they look up with the bright eyes of the outcast, fear

strokes the back of your neck, for you are the outcast now,
remembering the strangeness of stadium lights burning the sky,
the rattle of shoulder pads, the drumroll of cleats on pavement,
and the crowd rising and crying out in its great hunger
as you step onto that field of agony and endless promise.

Getting Fired

for Patti

Drunk now, you turn on some Billie Holiday
and dance with your wife, who is drunk, too,
because you called ahead. You say, I have written,
I have taught, among those who have not.
Ah, she says, but you did not wear a tie,
your shoes walked around unshined,
and your beard refused the loyalty oath.
Worst of all, your poems were blackballed
by the DAR. You have failed, my friend.

Your friend has her hand on the small
of your back, and you are feeling better now.
The voice of a woman who knew more pain
than any ten professors sings of love gone
wrong and the grace that follows loss.
The changes in a twelve-bar blues are open
doors to her, every chord a new way out.
On a diminished seventh *love*, she says, *love*,
and you pull the blinds, and begin to dance again.

On the Death of Small Towns: A Found Poem

from the *Seymour Daily Tribune,* Seymour, Indiana

Our little town grows smaller, and news from last week was spare.
Here is what I have to pass on.
Mrs. Josephine Baker of Elizabethtown and Mrs. Inez Loyd of
Seymour called at Winklepleck-Weesner Funeral home this
past Monday to pay their respects to Kelsa Cockerham.
I telephoned my oldest daughter, Mrs. Jan Stevenson, at La Porte,
Texas, last Thursday evening to wish her "Happy Birthday."
Sorry to hear of the death of Wayne Hendershot of St. Petersburg,
Fla., who passed away at Bayshore Hospital there. His
grandfather, the late Eliza Hendershot, built the house that
we moved here to. Wayne used to drive a huckster wagon
owned by Raymond Wilson of Surprise. He drove through the
community one day a week with about everything you would
find in a store.
Mrs. Frances Hockstetler of Brownstown visited her daughter,
Mrs. Marlin Timberlake, last Saturday to help Marlin celebrate
her birthday.
Sorry to hear of the death of Riley Perrin of Lexington, Ky., who
passed away at Central Baptist Hospital there Jan. 3. He was
the son of the late Dan and Fannie Scott Perrin of Brownstown.
Dan ran a shoe repair shop there for many years. I knew Riley
when he and his wife were here with his parents for a while
just before Mrs. Perrin passed away.
I received a telephone call Tuesday evening from my youngest
daughter, Mrs. Michaelee Nolen, from Anderson.
I read Dorothy (Perrin) Burns, of Ft. Worth, Texas, has been in the

hospital five times in the past year. She is the daughter of the late Mr. and Mrs. Dan Perrin and a sister to Riley Perrin, who recently passed away.

I attended the funeral of Kelsa Cockerham at Brownstone First Christian Church Monday.

Heard a flock of wild geese passing overhead on its way south Jan. 21. It was dark and I couldn't see them. I stood and listened till I couldn't hear them anymore. They surely knew

this cold was coming.

Leaving

My Chevy in gray primer, raked, coils cut,
lake pipes rumbling, and I'm gliding past
Debbie Lee's house, then the football field,
summer bindweed snaking up through
chicken wire, yard lines blown away,
the fullback's father who hasn't been right
since Korea waving from his porch swing,
then 3rd Street and the tin-roofed farmhouse
like the one in Oklahoma filled with lives that
made my life: my father tall beside his Ford,
my mother shy, leaning into him, *leaving,*

and now it's me, MOSELEY'S 66, JIM'S DINER,
drinking with the Imhoff twins from Hogtown
who leave next week for boot camp, and good-bye
to Main Street, the PLAZA, SHORTY'S RECREATION,
PAUL'S CAFE, where I bussed dishes and fell
in love with the waitress named LuAnn whose
light-filled hair came down one night for me,
but already I was gone, abandoning the lisp
of wheat stalks, deep fall into star-heaped
summer nights making love in the torn backseat,
quart beer bottles floating in the Cimarron,
cemetery's circle of Civil War graves where
we smoked our first weed and sang hymns,
and the library on Kansas Ave., returning late

again *The Story of Philosophy, Farewell
to Arms, Winesburg, Ohio, The Razor's Edge,
Spinoza's Ethics,* read but hardly understood,
who am I, what is a life, what is a good life,
the old questions, words that burn like headlights
lifting fields of red maize out of darkness and

me out of darkness three days after graduation,
sobered up, friends hugged and scattered,
COTTONWOOD LOUNGE in the rearview mirror
while ahead wait Plato, Aristotle, Dante,
Shakespeare, Keats, Melville, Dostoyevsky,
Fitzgerald, the blue lawn, the green light,
and a New World called *the life of the mind.*

for professors Frank Nelick, Dennis Quinn and John Senior

Swan Lake

for Elise Paschen

My sister led me by the hand
to the only movie house in Fairfax, Oklahoma,
where cottonwoods leaned over red-dirt streets
and the Osage lived in square houses.
We sat straight up in back-row seats,
our faces pale among brown skins.
We listened to strange syllables, stared
into dark eyes. We were surrounded.
The awful hush came crashing down
when an ancient phonograph
began to grind out *Swan Lake.*
From the wings the tallest woman in the world
stepped the way, I thought, a deer would
when it is alone. She raised her arms
and parted clouds. Her body
swept like rain across the broken stage.
A pirouette pulled the moon down low,
and when she leaped, the tide came in.
Around us rose small sighs and moans.
We watched an old woman weep
and hug her shawl. When the music stopped,
we saw a storm of people, hands held high,
and heard the sudden thunder of their cry,
TALLCHIEF   TALLCHIEF   TALLCHIEF,
the rumble of their feet against the floor
like a thousand buffalo beneath a darkening sky.

Obed Theodore Swearingen, 1883–1967

This is for O. T. Swearingen,
who loved bluegrass music
more than oil in the ground,
who played Moon and Forty-two
and shot rabbits farther than I could see,
whose constant friend was silence,
who was a stranger in church
and seldom spoke of God

but who one Oklahoma morning
looked down on me, hand on my shoulder,
his head crowned by the sun.

Rothko

Night shift on Rine #4 with three thousand feet of drill pipe
churning Oklahoma rock, the mud pump's wheeze and suck,
hammer of warped deck plates beneath my boot as I gaze
from the rig's north side upon treeless, dustbowl No Man's Land.
The moon slithers under clouds that go all sullen and spread
a great swath of indigo along the horizon, sinking to something
like the blue-black of threaded iron curling off a machine lathe.

Below, random bits of scarlet here and there bleeding through
a silver-gray band of town lights under dust and slung like
an oil rag over gas stations, bars, a doubleheader at the ball field,
workers' homes on the outskirts and lost farms scattered just beyond,
the house of my grandparents lifting then into memory behind
the burnished clods of plowed fields. And so five decades later deep
in the thrall of time's continuum, here I stand among the Rothkos

in Houston, city of my birth, thinking of the lives that came before
in all their colors—bruised blue fingernails, hands and wrists
gray with grease, jeans streaked with rust-red Panhandle clay—
and the lives that followed: my children, eyes blue or hazel, that peer
now into the darkening clouds of a mind drifting toward the far
horizon of colors, one upon another—*kadosh*, he might have said—
what the light gives back, and finally, what it doesn't. *Kadosh.*

A House

It's just a house. And standing on the sagging porch,
peering from the screen door through cramped, unlit rooms
to the sun-struck kitchen in back, I can finally make out
odd hunks of darkness drifting up—a dining table,
four chairs that weirdly look at first like monks at prayer,
flecks of some reflected distant glow or fire
scattered from a couch's plastic cover, the white keys
of an upright piano in its thick Victorian silence.
A small house, postwar, working people surely,
their lives of work buried in the vague odor of oil and sweat
rising from the carpet, whose green swirls twist into view.
A strange light begins to fill the front room's lace curtains,
falls like a fine dust, like mortality itself,
upon the Blue Willow dishware and the family photos
arranged around the Motorola's wire antenna.
And now so faintly, so terribly, voices float
from the kitchen, women's voices flute-like and sudden,
then little bursts of laughter, a flurry of whispers,
a sharp *No!,* and there he is, *there he is,* a small boy
standing in the kitchen door, surprised and smiling
the purest form of happiness, then walking quickly
toward me in his white T-shirt, jeans and blue
Brooklyn Dodgers cap, those bright hazel eyes looking up

and hands spread wide and raised against the screen
of the door, pushing, pushing hard until it opens,
its rusted spring creaking in that long cry that sounds
like a question without words, and I walk through.

Poem
(from *Early Occult Memory Systems of the Lower Midwest)*
(2003)

Poem

The name of the bow is life, but its work is death.
—FRAGMENTS

How in Heraclitus
ideas of things, quality, and event
coalesce—sun/warmth/dawn—
the perceiver/perceived, too,
not yet parsed, not yet,
and then the great Forgetting,
knower and known, love and beloved,
world and God-in-the-world.

But then it comes upon us: that brightness,
that bright tension in animals, for instance,
that focus, that compass
of the mammalian mind finding
its own true North,
saintly in its dark-eyed,
arrow-eared devotion.
A kind of calling, a *via negativa,*
a surrender, still and silent, to the heart's desire.

So in the cathedral of the world
we hold communion,
the bread of language
placed delicately upon our tongues
as we breathe the bitter air,
drinking the wine of reason
while lost, still, in the *mysterium* of Being.

NOTES

The Arrival of the Future

"Flight": This poem is a dramatic monologue inspired by a passage, used as an epigraph here, from George Steiner's essay, "Humane Literacy," in *Language and Silence* (New York: Atheneum, 1977, p. 11) in which Steiner is paraphrasing Dostoyevsky.

"Groceries": The lines quoted are from Louise Glück's poem, "The School Children," in *The House on Marshland* (New York: Ecco Press, 1975, p. 19).

The Art of the Lathe

"The Dumka": Dumka is the name of the second movement of the piano quintet, Op. 81 in A Major, mentioned in the poem.

"A Model of Downtown Los Angeles, 1940": Although the story of the Owens Valley/Los Angeles aqueduct is generally well known (and debated) in California, it may be less known elsewhere other than through the film *Chinatown,* which is not, obviously, a documentary but a drama loosely based on the incidents leading to the construction of the aqueduct. In 1905, encouraged by repeated headlines in the *Los Angeles Times* declaring a state of drought, citizens of Los Angeles voted for a bond issue to finance the building of an aqueduct from the Owens Valley 230 miles northeast of the city, a project of astonishing proportions successfully carried out by the brilliant, self-taught engineer, William Mulholland. But the aqueduct was brought not to Los Angeles but rather to the San Fernando Valley a few miles northwest of L.A., where a group known as the San Fernando Valley land syndicate—including the owner of the *Los Angeles Times,* Henry Huntington, Moses Sherman (a member of the L.A. water board), and other fabulously wealthy men—had purchased thousands of acres of cheap land that would now be worth tens of millions of dollars. Two years after construction was completed, the San Fernando Valley was annexed to Los Angeles (thus, Noah Cross's famous line in *Chinatown,* "Either you bring the water to L.A., or you bring L.A. to the water"). Over the years, the effect upon farmers in the Owens Valley was disastrous, but the economic benefit to L.A. was beyond measure; it would be fair to speculate that without the aqueduct L.A. today would be a small city about the size of Tulsa, Oklahoma. In my poem, the story is told from the point of view of a former resident (and victim) of the Owens Valley. Other references: *Gunga Din* (1939) was filmed in the Owens Valley. Franz Werfel, author of *Song of Bernadette* and friend of Kafka, was a part of the European émigré community in L.A. during the late thirties and forties, along with Mann and the others named here. Manzanar was a prison camp for Japanese U.S. citizens during World War II; the Rodney King beating, widely televised, culminated in the L.A. riots of 1992.

"The Art of the Lathe": Ramsden, Vauconson, and the others named here were major contributors to the development of the lathe and other machine tools. See W. Steeds, *A History of Machine Tools 1700–1910* (Oxford: Clarendon Press, 1969).

Early Occult Memory Systems of the Lower Midwest

"Moses Yellowhorse Is Throwing Water Balloons from the Hotel Roosevelt": Moses Yellowhorse played one and a half seasons for the Pittsburgh Pirates, 1921–1922, always listed on the roster as Chief Yellowhorse. The famous game in which he struck out Gehrig, Ruth, and Lazzeri in succession occurred during spring training.

"The Blue Buick": The Cendrars epigraph is my translation from the Folio reprint of the 1949 Denoël edition of *Le Lotissement du ciel* (*The Subdividing of the Sky*), edited and annotated by Claude Leroy, pp. 406–407:

> . . . je lisais les Classiques dans une édition anglaise; mais il m'arrivait aussi, toujours pour me distraire, de dérouler une carte du ciel sur la grande table et de recouvrir chaque constellation avec des pierres précieuses que j'allais quérir dans la réserve des coffres, marquant les étoiles de première grandeur avec les plus beaux diamants, complétant les figures avec les plus vivantes pierres de couleur remplissant les intervalles entre les dessins avec une coulee des plus belles perles de la collection de

Léouba, . . . Elles étaient toutes belles! Et je me récitais la page immortelle et pour moi inoubliable de Marbode sur la symbolique des pierres précieuses que je venais de découvrir dans *Le Latin mystique* de Rémy de Gourmont, ce livre gemmé, une compilation, une traduction, un anthologie, qui a bouleversé my conscience et m'a, en somme, baptisé ou, tout au moins, coverti à la Poésie, initié au Verbe, catéchisé.

In his notes, Leroy quotes Cendrars in *Bourlinguer*: "*Le Latin mystique* a été pour moi une date, une date de naissance intellectuelle." In his journal, Roy's first quote from the section of *Sky* entitled *Le ravissement d'amour* is his translation of "Le saint aussi a ses migraines et ses dégoûts de lassitude. . . . Il se méfie de l'illusion, du somnambulisme comme dans les rêves, des acrobaties comme chez certains intoxiqués et des attaques du haut mal, et des crises de nerfs comme chez certains épileptiques et névropathes" (p. 247). Roy's second quotation is also from that section: "L'oraison mentale est la volière de Dieu" (p. 244).

Roy's critique of Los Angeles refers to the construction of the Los Angeles Aqueduct, which, through "false droughts and artful title transactions" and the passing of a bond issue in 1905, diverted Owens River water from the Owens Valley and its farms and small towns and brought it 235 miles southwest to the San Fernando Valley, where Chandler and other members of two land syndicates had recently "bought or optioned virtually the entire valley." As Joan Didion further notes in *After Henry* (New York: Vintage, 1992), pp. 222–23:

> The extent to which Los Angeles was literally invented by the *Los Angeles Times* and by its owners, Harrison Gray Otis and his descendants in the Chandler family, remains hard for people in less recent parts of the country to fully comprehend. At the time Harrison Gray Otis bought his paper there were only five thousand people living in Los Angeles. There was no navigable river. . . . Los Angeles has water today because Harrison Gray Otis and his son-in-law Harry Chandler wanted it, and fought a series of outright water wars to get it.

"A Wall Map of Paris": The epigraph is from Sonnet XXVI in the Second Part of *The Sonnets to Orpheus* (New York: Modern Library, 1995), translated by Stephen Mitchell, pp. 512, 513. Mitchell's translation of the entire passage is "—Oh compose the criers, / harmonious god! let them wake resounding, / let their clear stream carry the head and the lyre."

Usher

"Usher": Known as the "master builder," Robert Moses, Arterial Coordinator of New York City, enjoyed unprecedented power as an urban designer, radically altering the landscape and urban sociology of the city through his mammoth freeway projects, including the Cross Bronx Expressway, the construction of which (from 1948 to 1963) destroyed hundreds of blue-collar and middle-class neighborhoods, many of them predominantly Jewish. Arguably two of the four or five most important Protestant theologians of the twentieth century, Paul Tillich and Reinhold Niebuhr taught at Union Theological Seminary in Manhattan during the 1950s. Tillich's most widely read works for a popular audience were *The Courage to Be* and *Dynamics of Faith*. "The Heraclitean way" refers to the statement in the fragments of Heraclitus that "the path up and down is one and the same." In his reference to the Isenheim Altarpiece in Colmar, France, at the Musée d'Unterlinden, Nathan is thinking of the right side panel depicting Christ risen from the tomb.

"The Cottonwood Lounge": George Cantor, German mathematician (1845–1918), created set theory as well as the very controversial theory of transfinite numbers. He died in a mental institution.

"Wittgenstein, Dying": "Trakl" refers, of course, to Georg Trakl, the Austrian poet, whom Wittgenstein admired and to whom he gave a small portion of his inheritance though he confessed himself unable fully to understand Trakl's poems. Although World War One was "the nightmare of the earth" for all involved (and through a long line of historical connections continues to be), it was especially so for Trakl, who died from a cocaine overdose in 1914. Wittgenstein's *On Certainty* was written partially in response to G. E. Moore's argument against skepticism, which begins with Moore holding up one hand, pointing to it with the other, and saying, "This is one hand." "Paul" is Paul Wittgenstein, Ludwig's brother, a concert pianist who lost his right arm in World War One but continued performing, commissioning works for the left hand from such composers as Ravel, Strauss, and Britten.

"Gödel": Kurt Gödel, Czech-born American mathematician and philosopher, who worked with Einstein at the Princeton Institute for Advance Study, was best known for his incompleteness theorems. Nowhere did Gödel say that "no life contains its own clear validation"; that is solely Ira Campbell's inference. "Lansky" refers to Meyer Lansky, the legendary American mobster known especially for his financial shrewdness.

"The Beauty of Abandoned Towns": My loose, colloquial translation of the Latin epigraph is, "Work defeated everything, back-breaking work, and the grinding need of hard times."

"Nathan Gold": The American Objectivist poet, Charles Reznikoff, published his long poem, *Holocaust,* in 1975. Material for the poem was based upon transcriptions of court proceedings of the Nuremburg trial and the Eichmann trial. Eichmann's "use" of Kant is discussed at length in Hannah Arendt's *Eichmann in Jerusalem.* The *Malach HaMavet* is the Hebrew angel of death.

Hart Crane's lines quoted here are from the final two stanzas of "To Brooklyn Bridge":

> *Under thy shadow by the piers I waited;*
> *Only in darkness is thy shadow clear.*
> *The City's fiery parcels all undone,*
> *Already snow submerges an iron year . . .*

> *O Sleepless as the river under thee,*
> *Vaulting the sea, the prairies' dreaming sod,*
> *Unto us lowliest sometime sweep, descend*
> *And of the Curveship lend a myth to God.*

"Maria": Maria Rasputin, oldest daughter of the infamous Grigori Rasputin. "The mansion of the Railroad King" refers to the Huntington Library in Pasadena, California, a center for research on the poet William Blake. Alexandre Kojève (1902–1968) was a French philosopher born in Russia who exerted an immense influence on both European and American intellectuals, including the political philosopher, Leo Strauss; Alan Bloom (Strauss's student who later studied with Kojève); Bloom's student, Francis Fukuyama; and many others in both academic and political life. Fukuyama's book, *The End of History and the Last Man,* incorporated ideas and themes from Kojève.

"Poem": Formerly entitled "The Problem" and owing much to Professor Richard McKirahan's classes on Heraclitus at Pomona College and to Philip Wheelwright's commentary on the Fragments in *Heraclitus* (Oxford University Press, 1959), in particular this comment on Fragment Six: ". . . there is at least an overtone of suggestion that we come to know reality not by merely knowing about it . . . but by becoming of its nature." I am also indebted to comments on Parmenides and on Stephen MacKenna's famous translation of Plotinus which were given in a lecture by Donald Sheehan at the Frost Place, Franconia, New Hampshire, in August 2001.

ACKNOWLEDGMENTS

Grateful acknowledgment is made for poems in "New Poems" which originally appeared (although, in some cases, in different form or under different title) in the following publications:

Christianity and Literature: "The Death of a Gerbil"

The Cortland Review: "The Left Fielder's Sestina."

Green Mountains Review: "The End of Art"

Gulf Stream: "The Student Assistant"

Image: "Rothko"

Luvina (Mexico): "The Language of the Future"

Mississippi Review: "The Attaché Case"

New Letters: "Alzheimer's," "Dust Storm, No Man's Land, 1952," "Shakespeare in the Park, 9/11/2011"

Outerbridge: "Swan Lake"

Ploughshares: "The Game," "A House"

Provincetown Arts: "Abandoned Grain Elevator"

REAL: "Getting Fired," "Obed Theodore Swearingen, 1883–1967"

River Styx: "Language"

Salt Hill Journal: "Leaving"

Southern Poetry Review: "Betty"

The Virginia Quarterly Review: "Economics," "Three Girls Tossing Rings"

The Warwick Review (England): "The Men on Figueroa Street, Los Angeles, 1975," "Pale from the Hand of the Child That Holds It"

Yale Review: "Red Snow," "The Story."

"The Story" also appeared in the 2014 PushcartPrize anthology.

"The Student Assistant" was included in *Best of the Net 2010*.

This is my fourth book with W. W. Norton since Jill Bialosky invited me to submit the manuscript of *Early Occult Memory Systems of the Lower Midwest*. She has been a consistently supportive, efficient, and gracious editor, for which I am deeply appreciative. Many thanks, too, to Rebecca Schultz for her expertise and hard work on this project.